Originally launched on Facebook, Rupert Fawcett's brilliantly observed, touchingly truthful Off The Leash cartoons have developed a huge daily following around the world.

His *Off The Leash* books, *The Secret Life of Dogs*, *A Dog's Best Friend* and now *It's a Dog's Life*, bring together the very best of those cartoons, featuring the secret thoughts and conversations of dogs of every size, shape and breed. They are a celebration of our favourite belly-scratching, tail-chasing, bed-stealing canine friends – for dog lovers everywhere.

Also by Rupert Fawcett

Off The Leash: The Secret Life of Dogs
Off The Leash: A Dog's Best Friend

Off The Leash

IT'S A DOG'S LIFE

Rupert Fawcett

BOXTREE

First published 2015 by Boxtree
an imprint of Pan Macmillan
20 New Wharf Road, London N1 9RR
Associated companies throughout the world
www.panmacmillan.com

ISBN 978-0-7522-6574-2

Pan Macmillan does not have any control over, or any responsibility for,
any author or third party websites referred to in or on this book.

1 3 5 7 9 8 6 4 2

A CIP catalogue record for this book is available from the British Library.

Printed and bound in China

Visit **www.panmacmillan.com** to read more about all our books
and to buy them. You will also find features, author interviews and
news of any author events, and you can sign up for e-newsletters
so that you're always first to hear about our new releases.

Foreword

I was brought up with dogs and have always found them comical as well as adorable. I started drawing dog cartoons and posting them on Facebook in March 2012 and was amazed at the response; people from all over the world started sending me messages and photographs of their dogs re-enacting my cartoons. In a short period of time, what had started as a bit of fun grew into a full-time occupation.

My previous Off The Leash books, *The Secret Life of Dogs* and *A Dog's Best Friend*, have now been translated into several languages and proved to me that the love of dogs and their antics is truly universal. *It's a Dog's Life* is my third compilation in the series and once again features the inner workings of the minds of our favourite, adorable, needy and manipulative four-legged friends. I hope you enjoy reading it as much as I enjoyed drawing it.

Rupert Fawcett

For my mother, Pam Fawcett

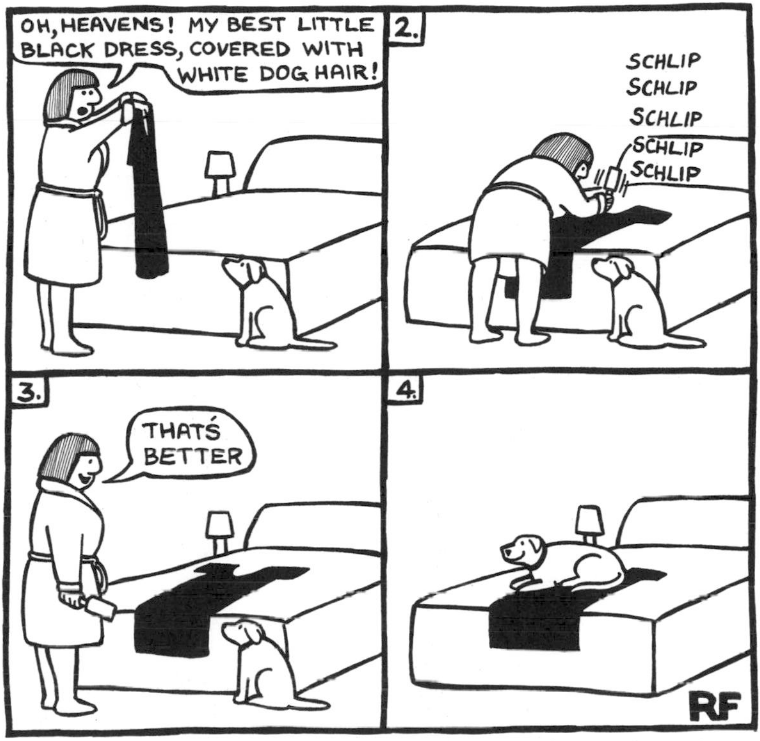

OH, HEAVENS! MY BEST LITTLE BLACK DRESS, COVERED WITH WHITE DOG HAIR!
2.
SCHLIP
SCHLIP
SCHLIP
SCHLIP
SCHLIP
3.
THATŚ BETTER
4.
RF

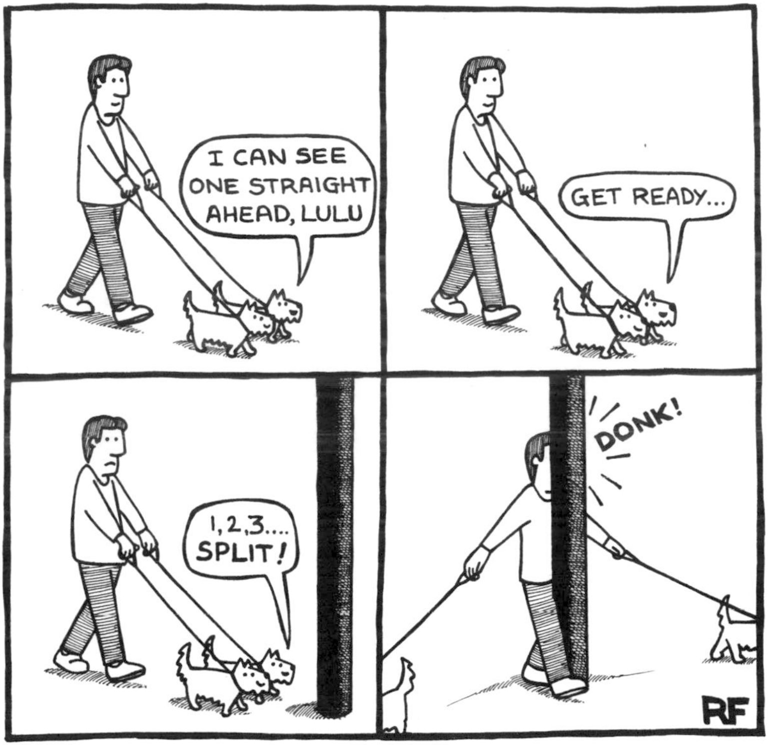
I CAN SEE ONE STRAIGHT AHEAD, LULU
GET READY...
1,2,3.... SPLIT!
DONK!
RF

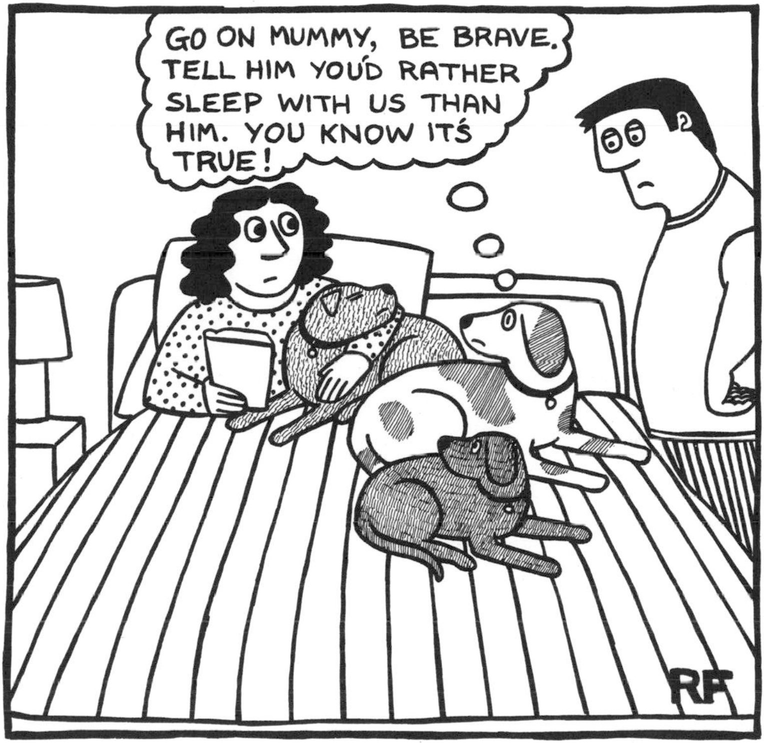
GO ON MUMMY, BE BRAVE. TELL HIM YOU'D RATHER SLEEP WITH US THAN HIM. YOU KNOW IT'S TRUE!
RF

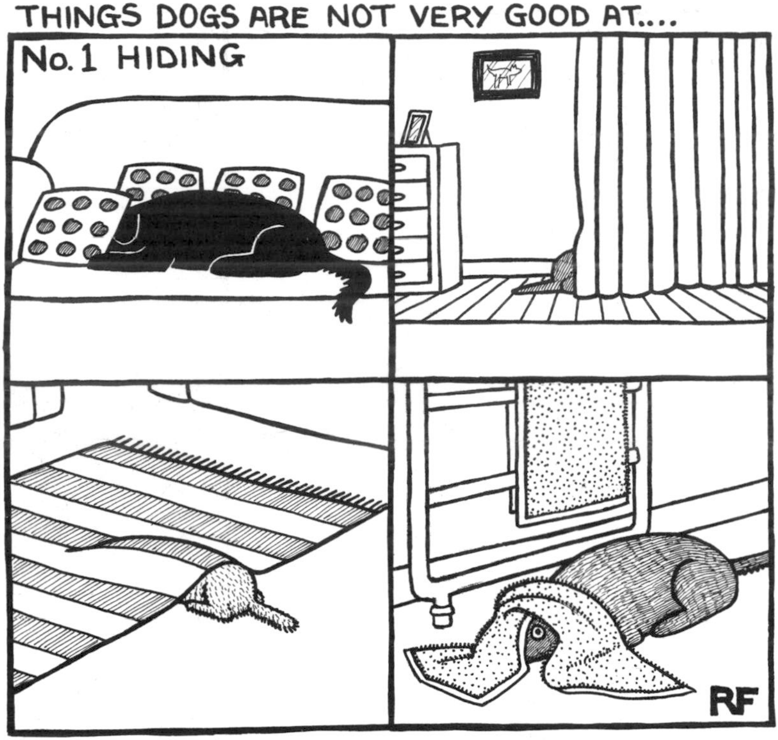
THINGS DOGS ARE NOT VERY GOOD AT....
No. 1 HIDING
RF

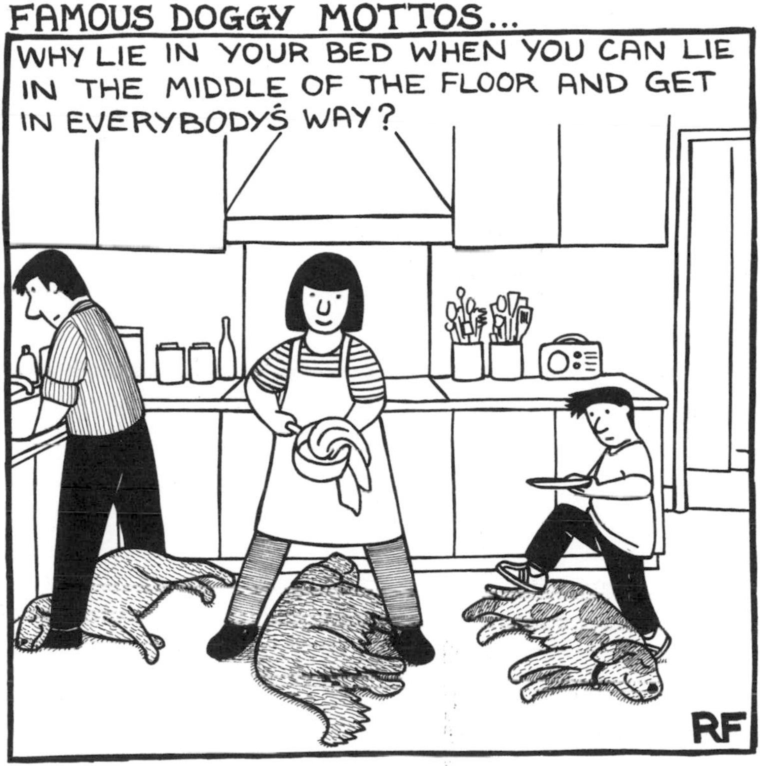
FAMOUS DOGGY MOTTOS...
WHY LIE IN YOUR BED WHEN YOU CAN LIE IN THE MIDDLE OF THE FLOOR AND GET IN EVERYBODY'S WAY?
RF

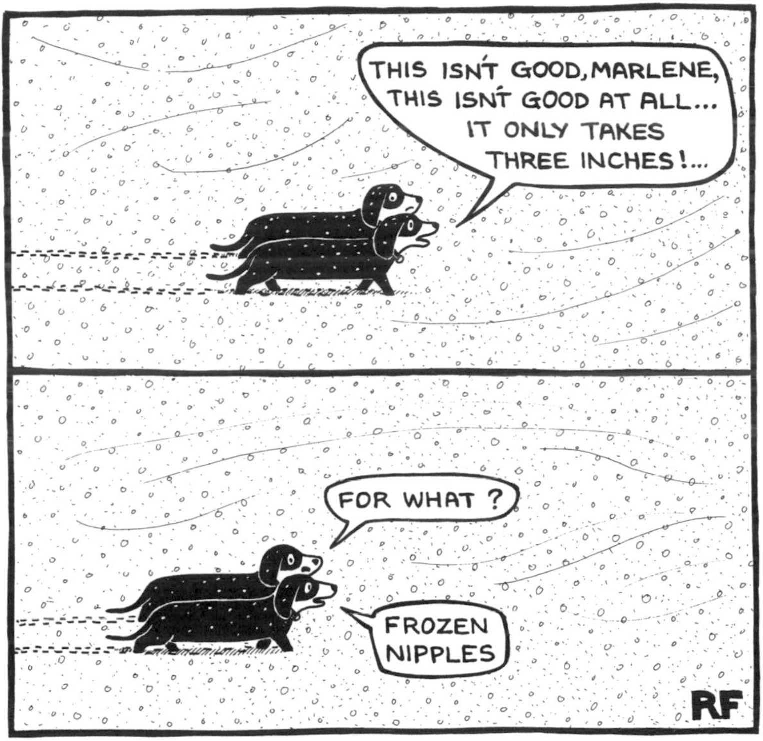
THIS ISN'T GOOD, MARLENE, THIS ISN'T GOOD AT ALL... IT ONLY TAKES THREE INCHES!...
FOR WHAT ?
FROZEN NIPPLES
RF

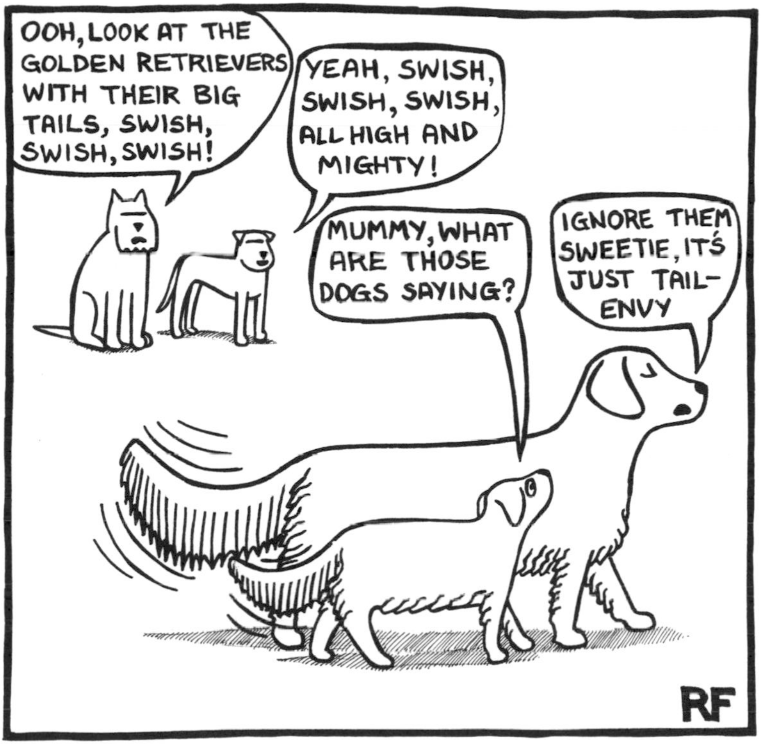
OOH, LOOK AT THE GOLDEN RETRIEVERS WITH THEIR BIG TAILS, SWISH, SWISH, SWISH!
YEAH, SWISH, SWISH, SWISH, ALL HIGH AND MIGHTY!
MUMMY, WHAT ARE THOSE DOGS SAYING?
IGNORE THEM SWEETIE, IT'S JUST TAIL-ENVY
RF

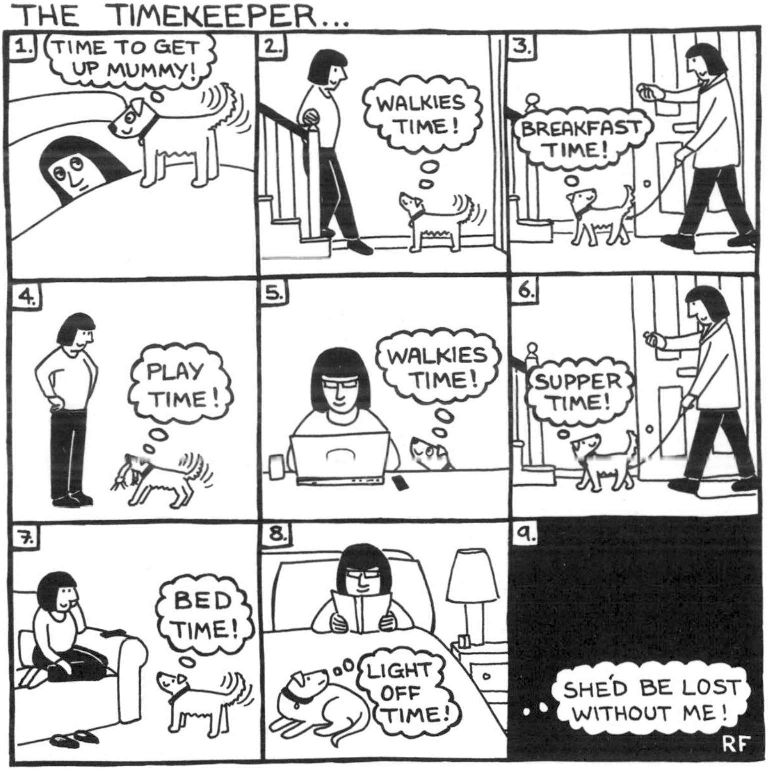
THE TIMEKEEPER...
1.
TIME TO GET UP MUMMY!
2.
WALKIES TIME!
3.
BREAKFAST TIME!
4.
PLAY TIME!
5.
WALKIES TIME!
6.
SUPPER TIME!
7.
BED TIME!
8.
LIGHT OFF TIME!
9.
SHE'D BE LOST WITHOUT ME!
RF

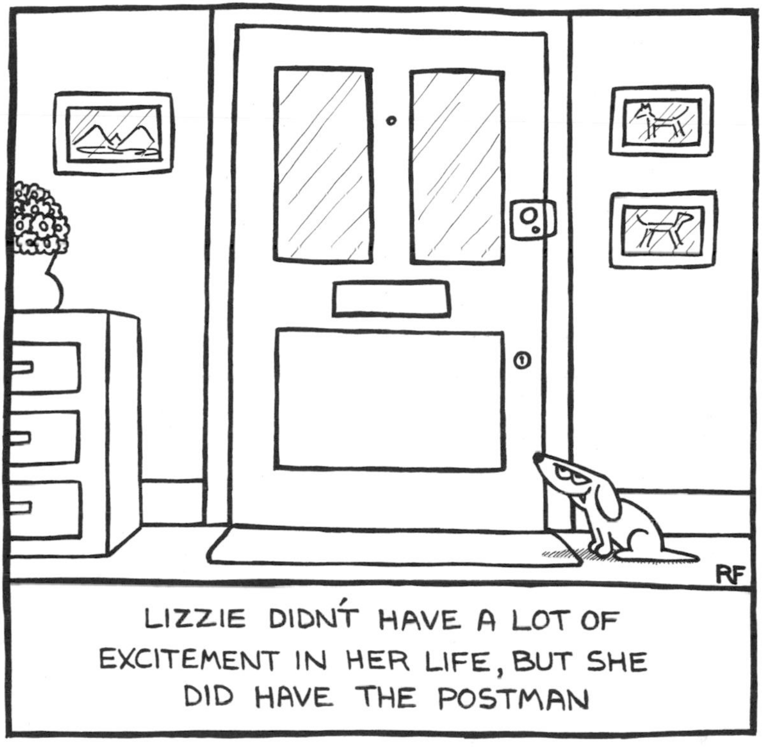
1
RF

LIZZIE DIDN'T HAVE A LOT OF EXCITEMENT IN HER LIFE, BUT SHE DID HAVE THE POSTMAN

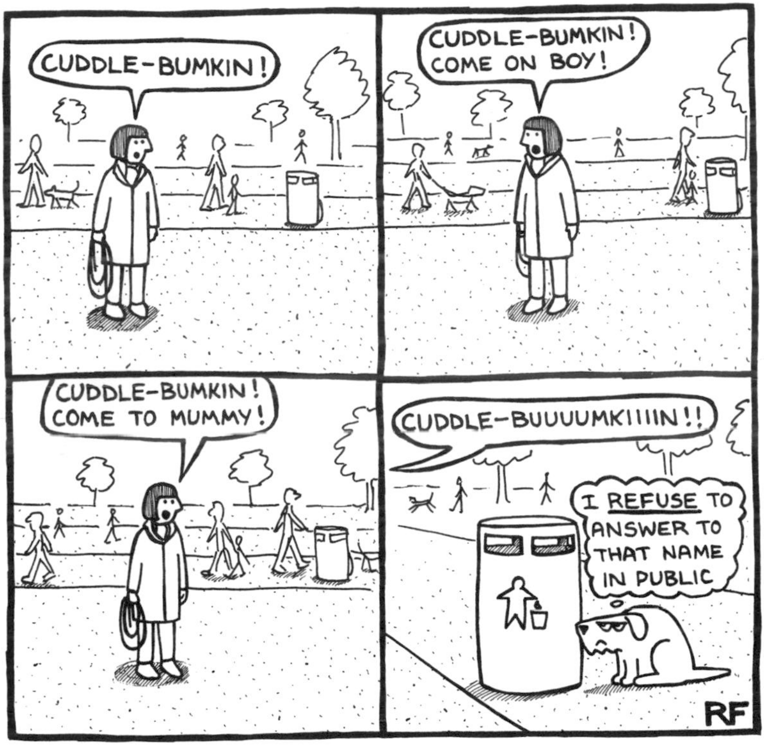
CUDDLE-BUMKIN!
CUDDLE-BUMKIN! COME ON BOY!
CUDDLE-BUMKIN! COME TO MUMMY!
CUDDLE-BUUUUMKIIIIN!!
I REFUSE TO ANSWER TO THAT NAME IN PUBLIC
RF

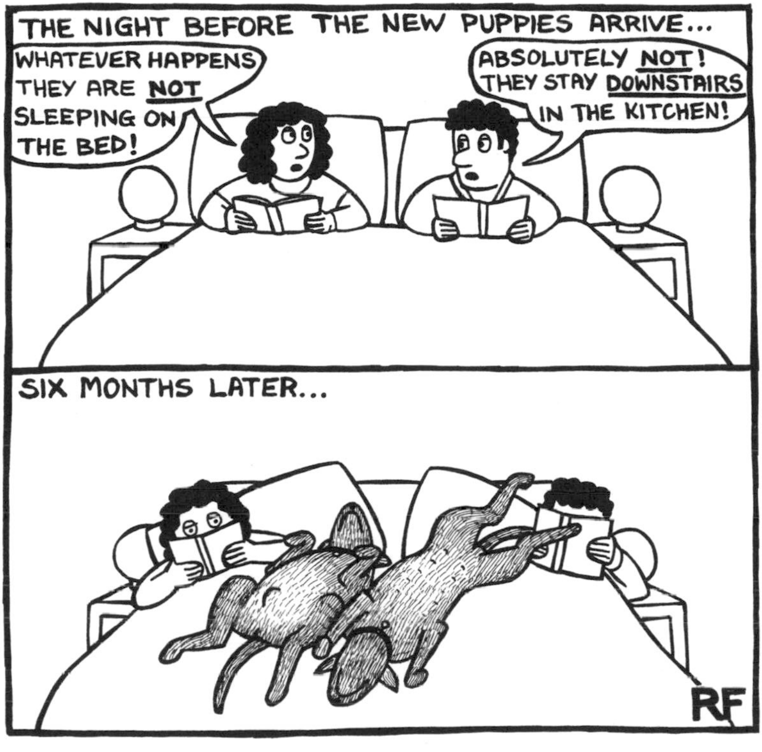
THE NIGHT BEFORE THE NEW PUPPIES ARRIVE...
WHATEVER HAPPENS THEY ARE NOT SLEEPING ON THE BED!
ABSOLUTELY NOT! THEY STAY DOWNSTAIRS IN THE KITCHEN!
SIX MONTHS LATER...
RF

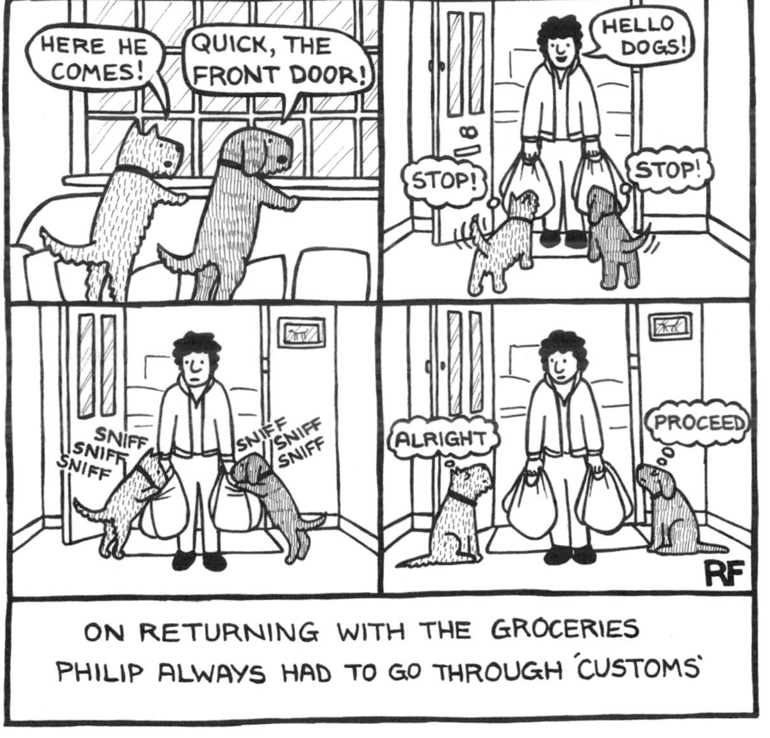
HERE HE COMES!
QUICK, THE FRONT DOOR!
HELLO DOGS!
STOP!
STOP!
SNIFF SNIFF SNIFF
SNIFF SNIFF SNIFF
ALRIGHT
PROCEED
RF

ON RETURNING WITH THE GROCERIES PHILIP ALWAYS HAD TO GO THROUGH 'CUSTOMS'

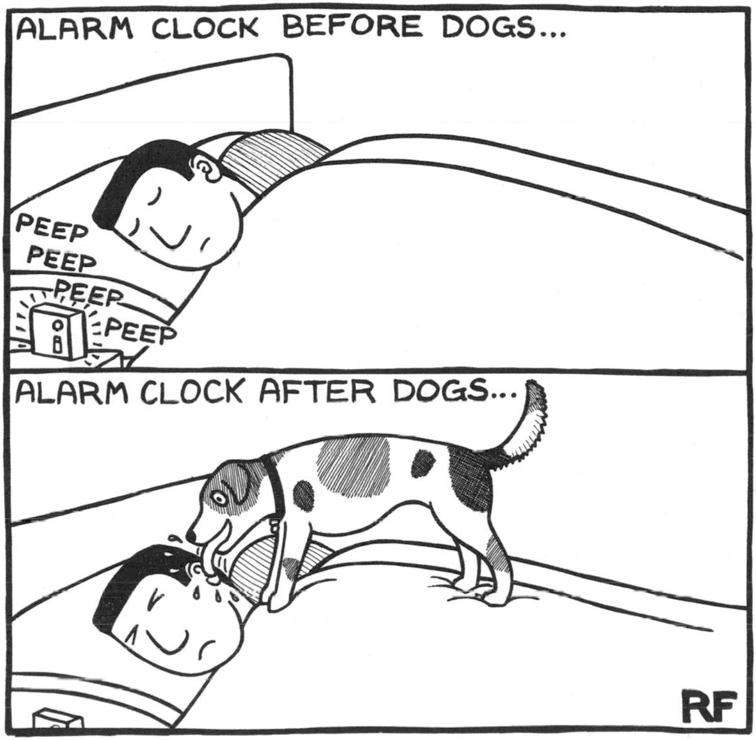
ALARM CLOCK BEFORE DOGS...
PEEP
PEEP
PEEP
PEEP
ALARM CLOCK AFTER DOGS...
RF

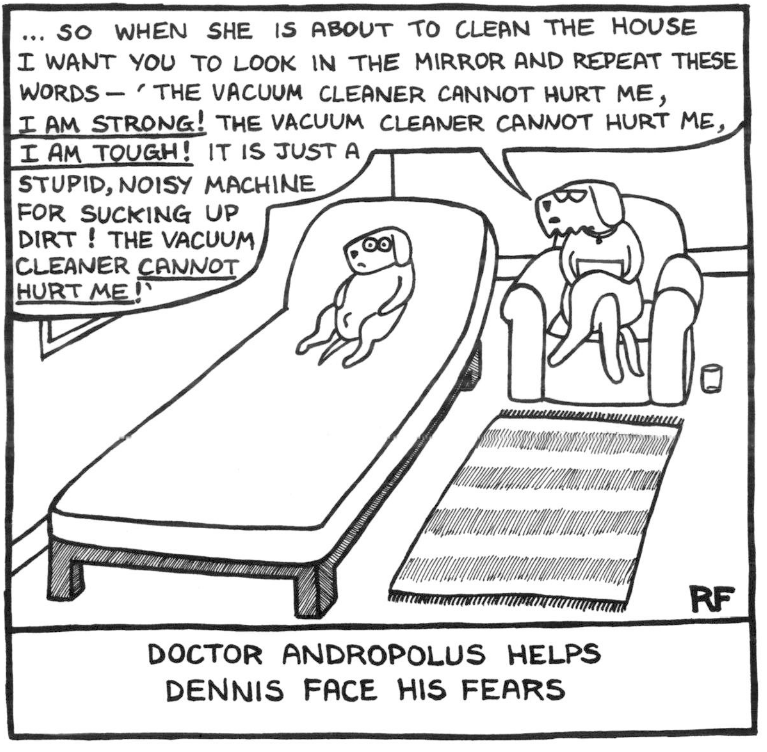
... SO WHEN SHE IS ABOUT TO CLEAN THE HOUSE I WANT YOU TO LOOK IN THE MIRROR AND REPEAT THESE WORDS – 'THE VACUUM CLEANER CANNOT HURT ME, I AM STRONG! THE VACUUM CLEANER CANNOT HURT ME, I AM TOUGH! IT IS JUST A STUPID, NOISY MACHINE FOR SUCKING UP DIRT! THE VACUUM CLEANER CANNOT HURT ME!'
RF

DOCTOR ANDROPOLUS HELPS DENNIS FACE HIS FEARS

ANOTHER BUSY DAY...
1.
2.
3.
4.
5.
6.
7.
8.
9.
RF

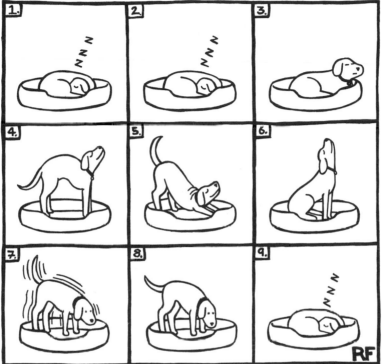

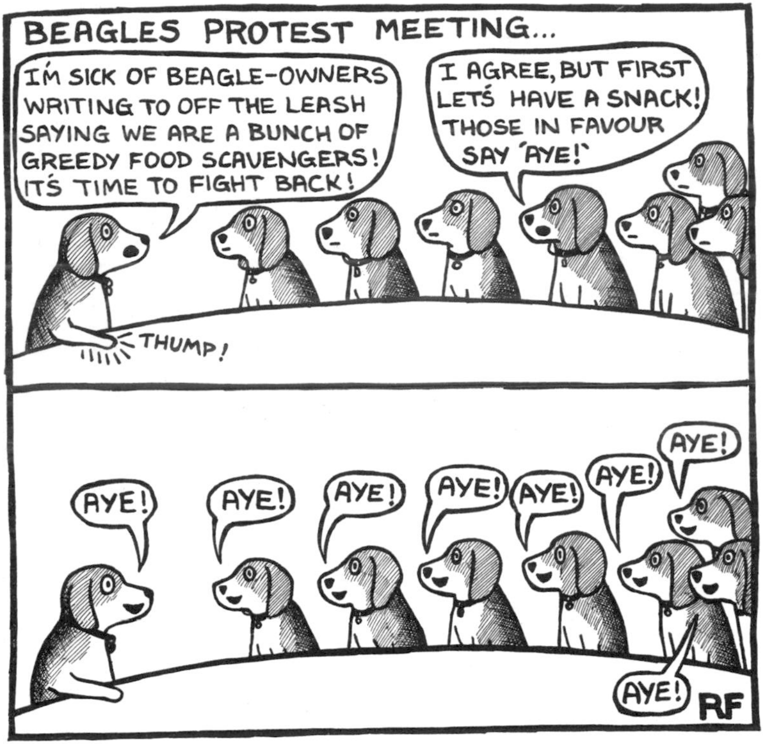
BEAGLES PROTEST MEETING...
I'M SICK OF BEAGLE-OWNERS WRITING TO OFF THE LEASH SAYING WE ARE A BUNCH OF GREEDY FOOD SCAVENGERS! IT'S TIME TO FIGHT BACK!
THUMP!
I AGREE, BUT FIRST LET'S HAVE A SNACK! THOSE IN FAVOUR SAY 'AYE!'
AYE!
AYE!
AYE!
AYE!
AYE!
AYE!
AYE!
AYE!
RF

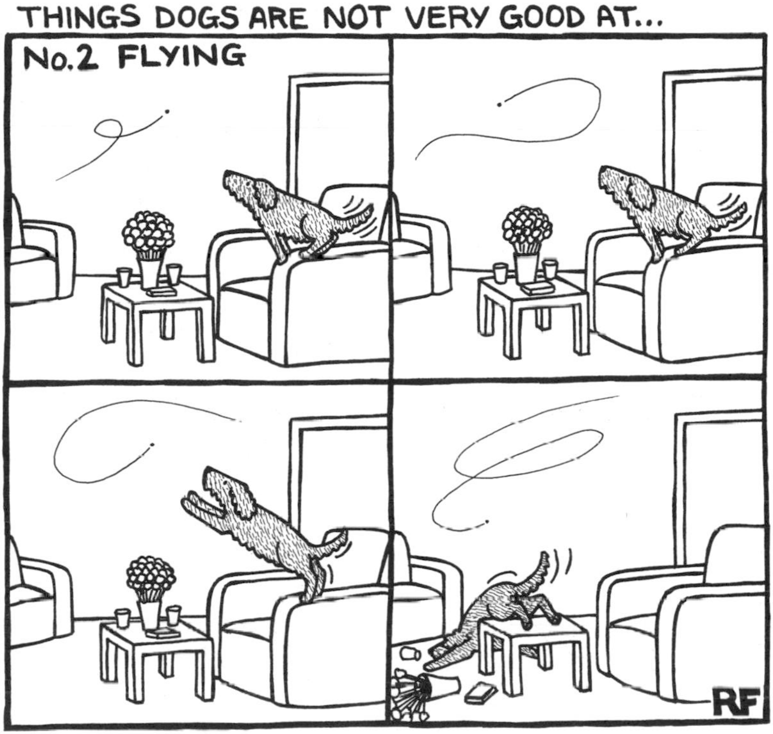
THINGS DOGS ARE NOT VERY GOOD AT...
No.2 FLYING
RF

A QUIET NIGHT IN FRONT OF THE TV...

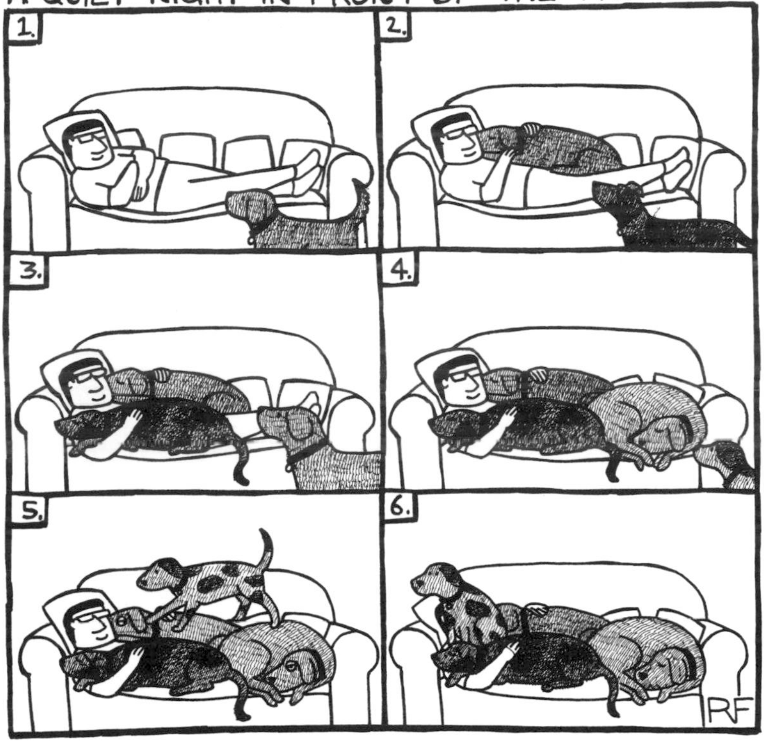

1.
2.
3.
4.
5.
6.
RF

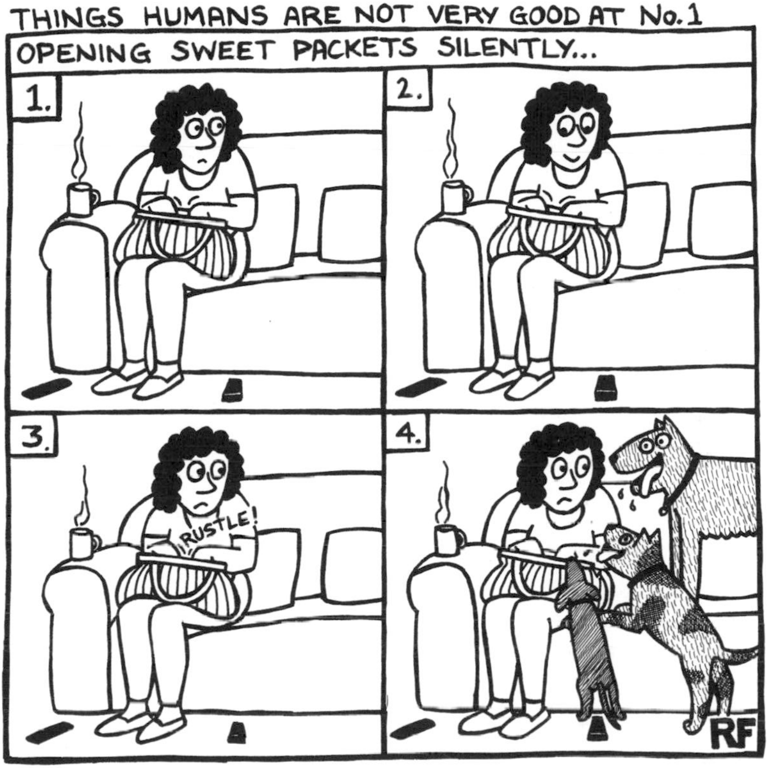
THINGS HUMANS ARE NOT VERY GOOD AT No.1
OPENING SWEET PACKETS SILENTLY...
1.
2.
3.
RUSTLE!
4.
RF

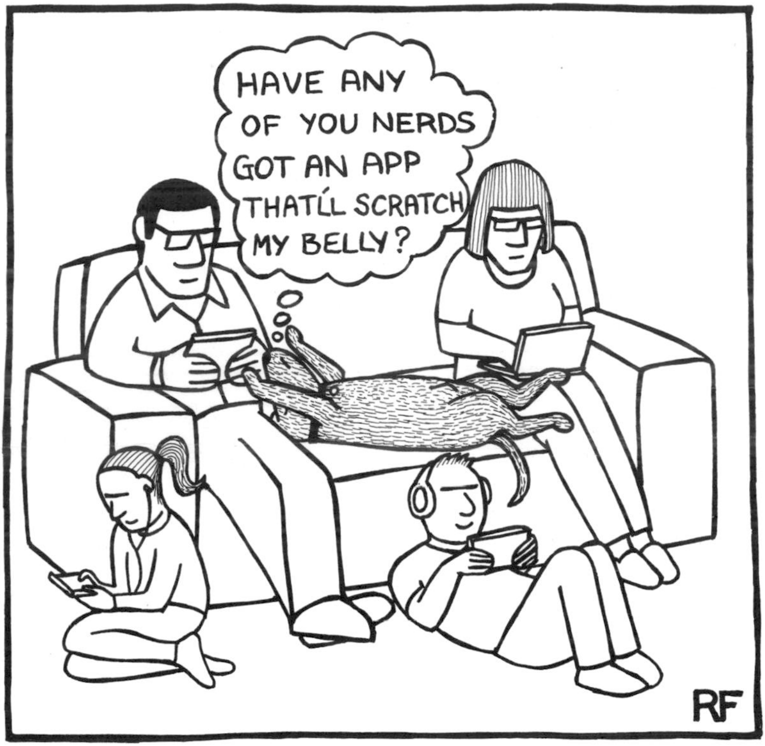
HAVE ANY OF YOU NERDS GOT AN APP THATĹL SCRATCH MY BELLY?
RF

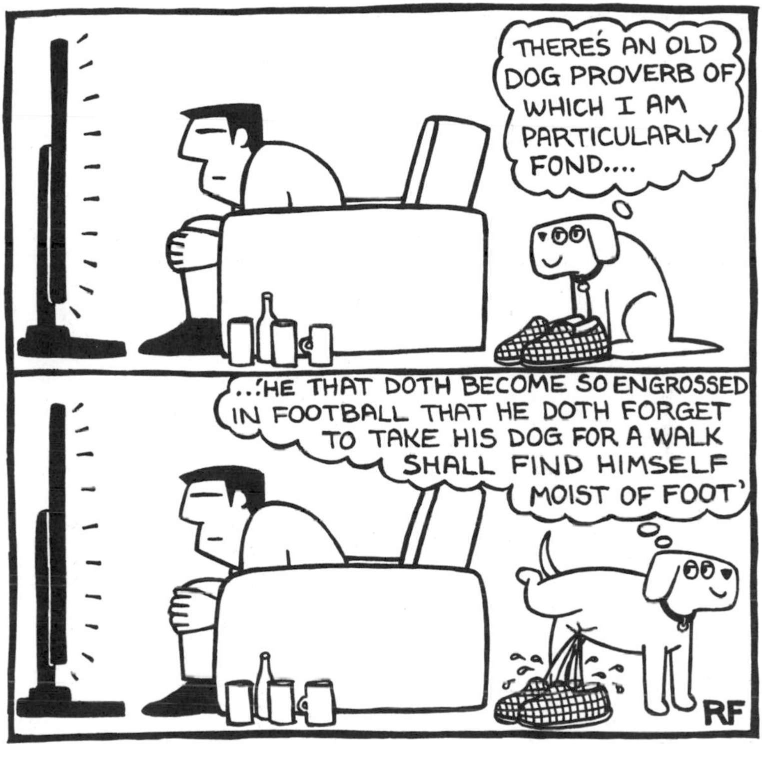
THERE'S AN OLD DOG PROVERB OF WHICH I AM PARTICULARLY FOND....
...'HE THAT DOTH BECOME SO ENGROSSED IN FOOTBALL THAT HE DOTH FORGET TO TAKE HIS DOG FOR A WALK SHALL FIND HIMSELF MOIST OF FOOT'
RF

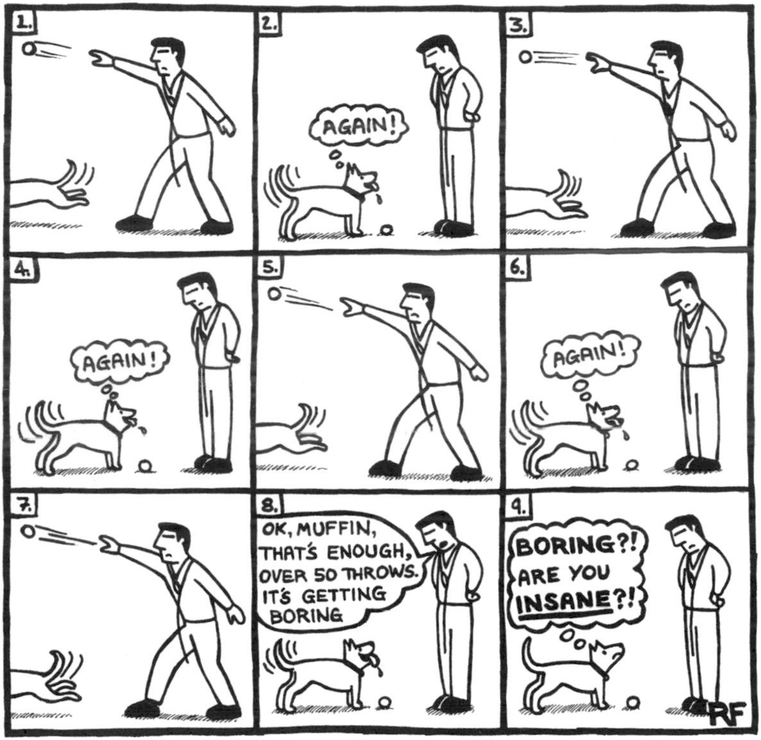
1.
2.
AGAIN!
3.
4.
AGAIN!
5.
6.
AGAIN!
7.
8.
OK, MUFFIN, THAT'S ENOUGH, OVER 50 THROWS. IT'S GETTING BORING
9.
BORING?! ARE YOU INSANE?!
RF

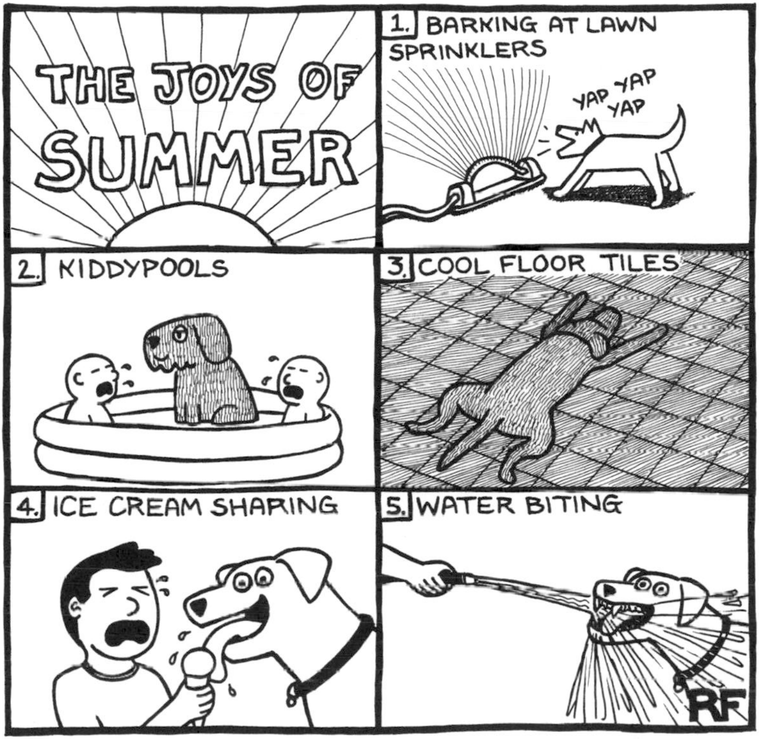
THE JOYS OF SUMMER
1. BARKING AT LAWN SPRINKLERS
YAP YAP YAP
2. KIDDYPOOLS
3. COOL FLOOR TILES
4. ICE CREAM SHARING
5. WATER BITING
RF

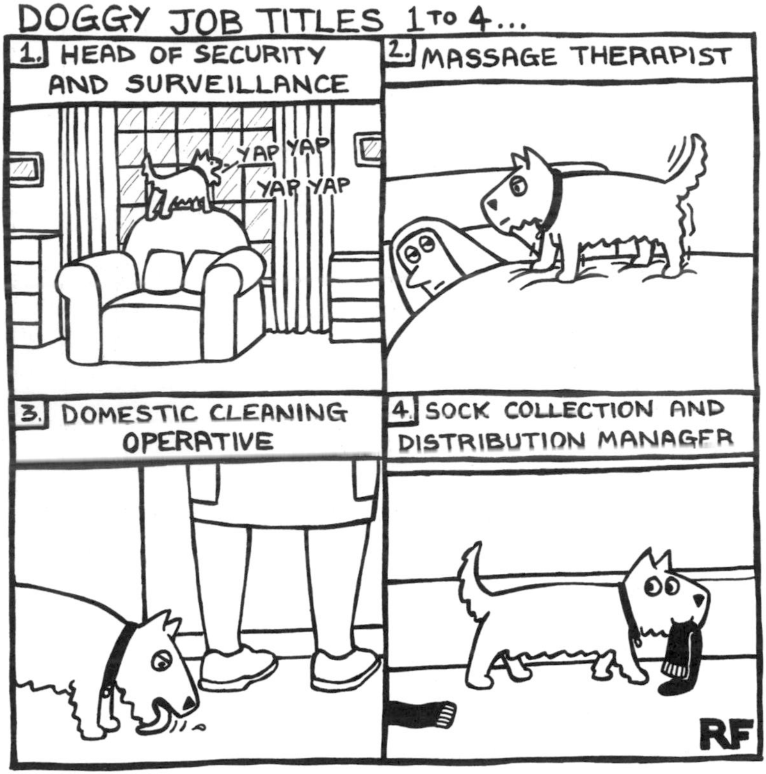
DOGGY JOB TITLES 1 TO 4...
1. HEAD OF SECURITY AND SURVEILLANCE
YAP YAP
YAP YAP
2. MASSAGE THERAPIST
3. DOMESTIC CLEANING OPERATIVE
4. SOCK COLLECTION AND DISTRIBUTION MANAGER
RF

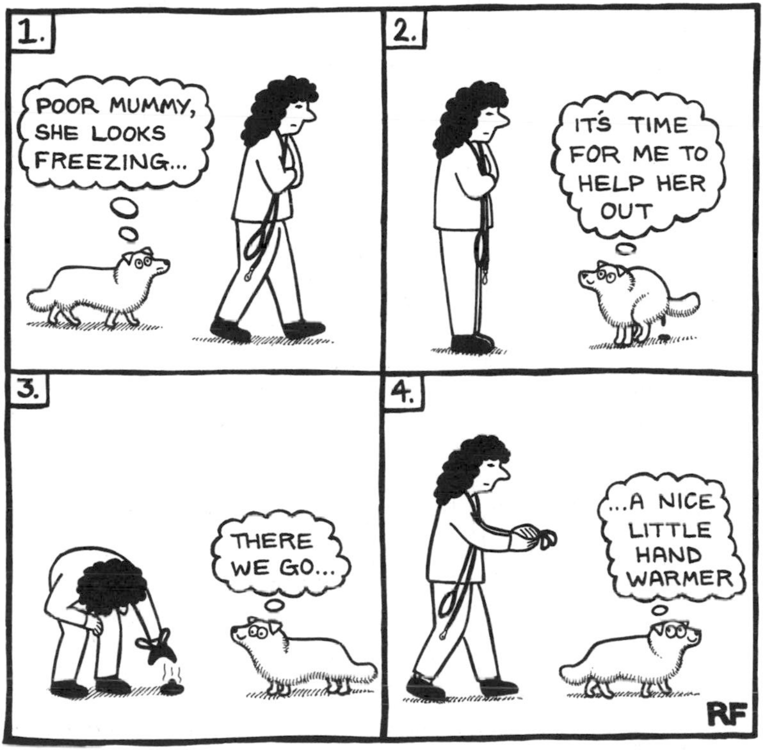
1.
POOR MUMMY, SHE LOOKS FREEZING...
2.
IT'S TIME FOR ME TO HELP HER OUT
3.
THERE WE GO...
4.
...A NICE LITTLE HAND WARMER
RF

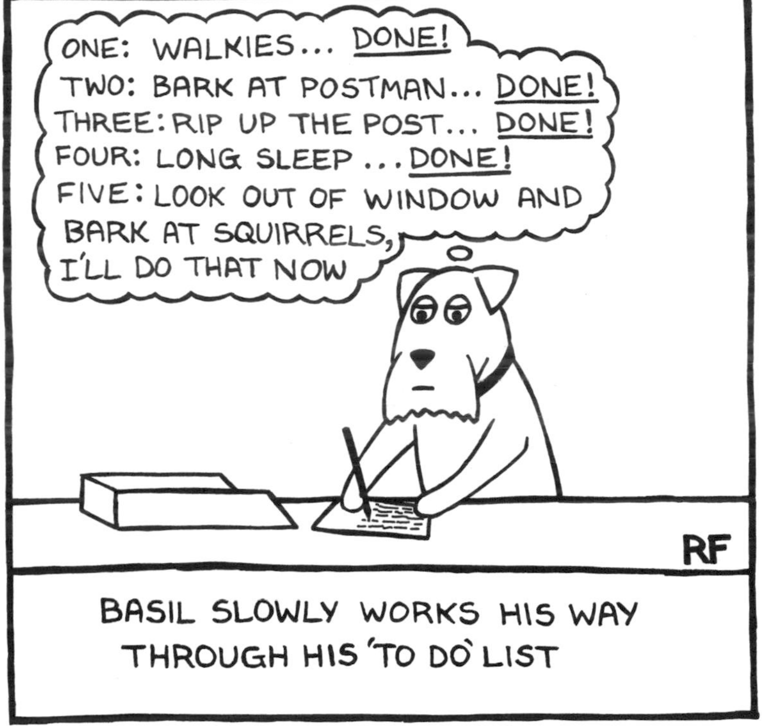
ONE: WALKIES... DONE!
TWO: BARK AT POSTMAN... DONE!
THREE: RIP UP THE POST... DONE!
FOUR: LONG SLEEP ... DONE!
FIVE: LOOK OUT OF WINDOW AND BARK AT SQUIRRELS, I'LL DO THAT NOW
RF

BASIL SLOWLY WORKS HIS WAY THROUGH HIS 'TO DO' LIST

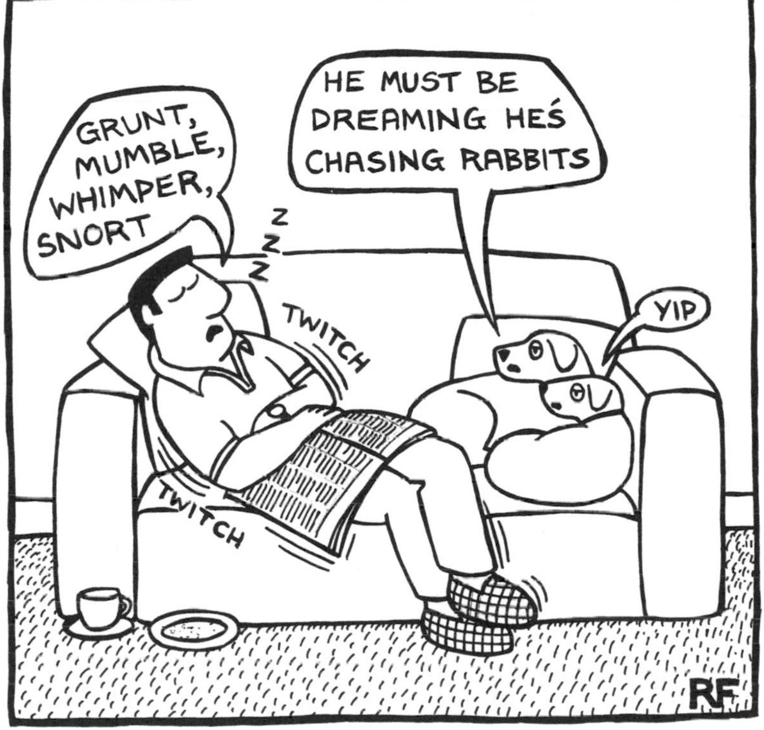
GRUNT, MUMBLE, WHIMPER, SNORT
Z Z Z
HE MUST BE DREAMING HEŚ CHASING RABBITS
TWITCH
YIP
TWITCH
RF

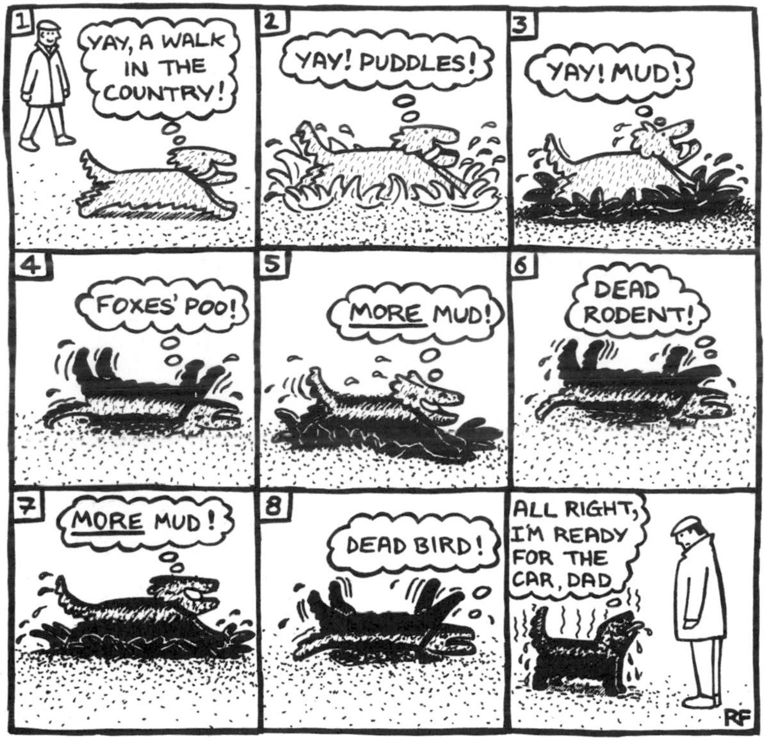
1
YAY, A WALK IN THE COUNTRY!
2
YAY! PUDDLES!
3
YAY! MUD!
4
FOXES' POO!
5
MORE MUD!
6
DEAD RODENT!
7
MORE MUD!
8
DEAD BIRD!
ALL RIGHT, I'M READY FOR THE CAR, DAD
RF

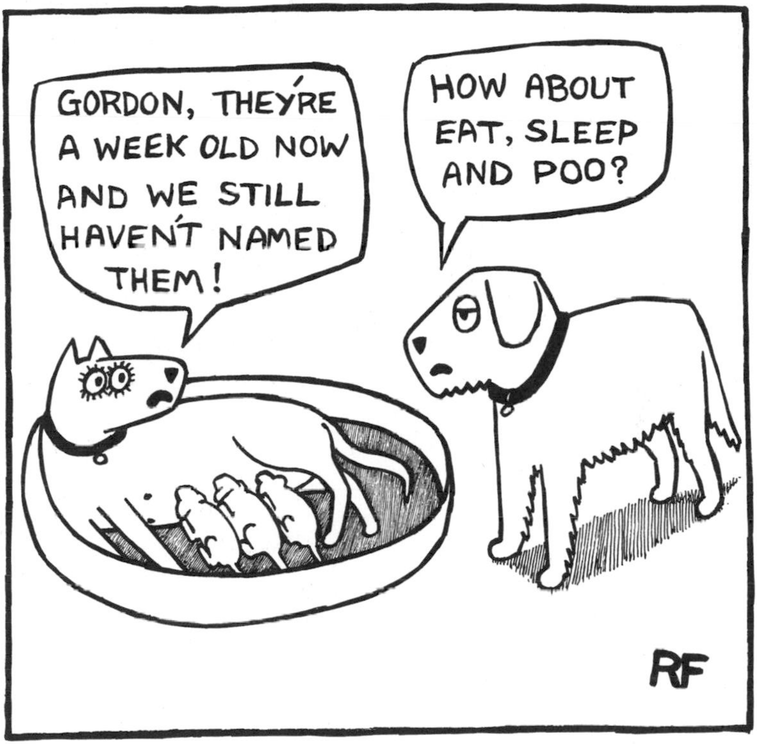
GORDON, THEY'RE A WEEK OLD NOW AND WE STILL HAVEN'T NAMED THEM!
HOW ABOUT EAT, SLEEP AND POO?
RF

THINGS HUMANS ARE NOT VERY GOOD AT No. 2

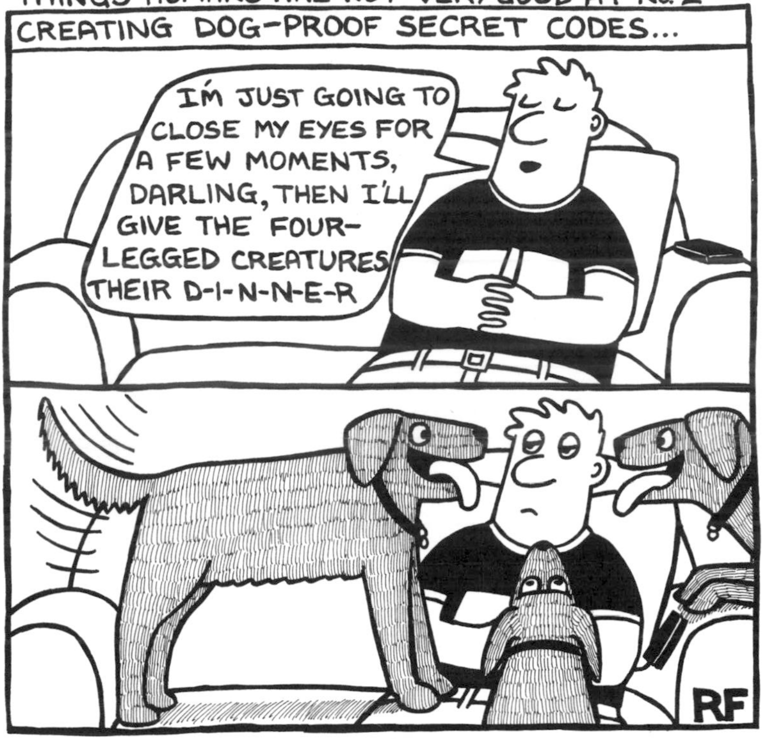
CREATING DOG-PROOF SECRET CODES...
I'M JUST GOING TO CLOSE MY EYES FOR A FEW MOMENTS, DARLING, THEN I'LL GIVE THE FOUR-LEGGED CREATURES THEIR D-I-N-N-E-R
RF

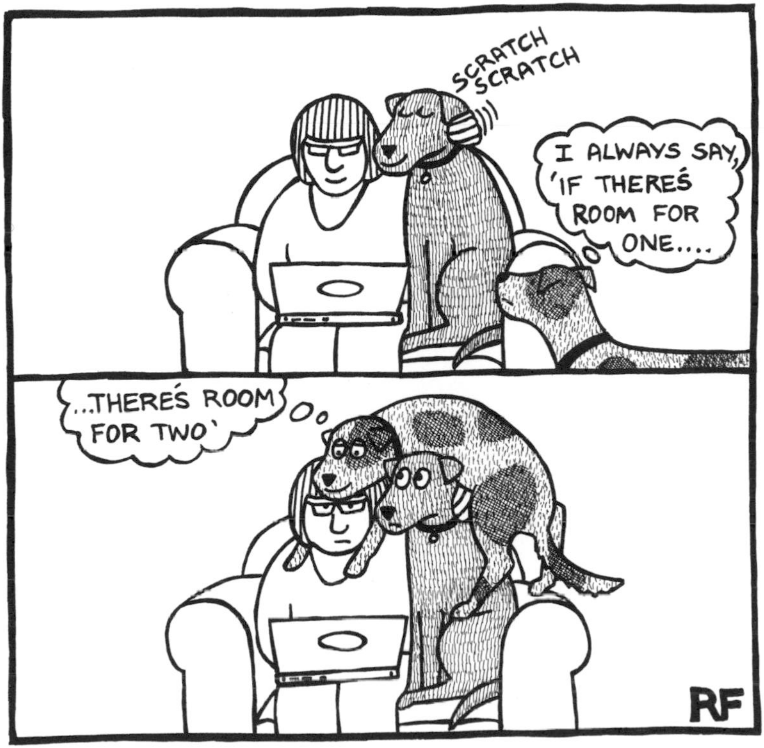
SCRATCH SCRATCH
I ALWAYS SAY, 'IF THERE'S ROOM FOR ONE....
...THERE'S ROOM FOR TWO'
RF

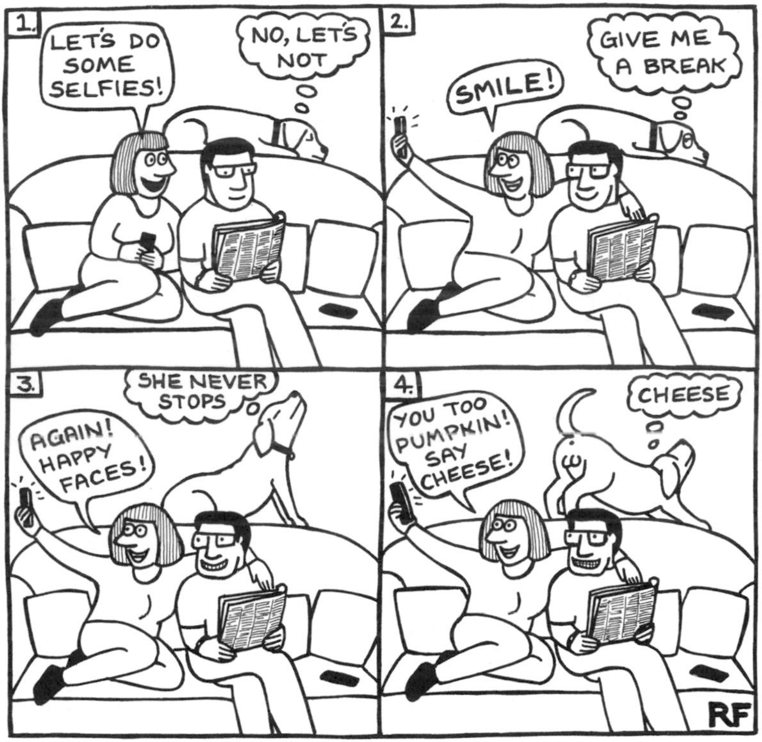
1.
LET'S DO SOME SELFIES!
NO, LET'S NOT
2.
SMILE!
GIVE ME A BREAK
3.
SHE NEVER STOPS
AGAIN! HAPPY FACES!
4.
YOU TOO PUMPKIN! SAY CHEESE!
CHEESE
RF

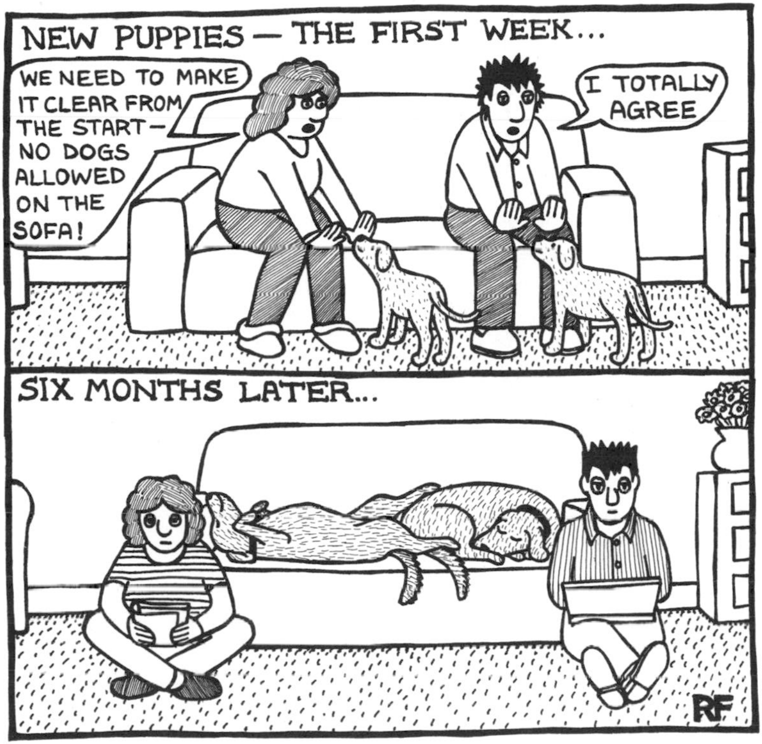
NEW PUPPIES — THE FIRST WEEK...
WE NEED TO MAKE IT CLEAR FROM THE START — NO DOGS ALLOWED ON THE SOFA!
I TOTALLY AGREE
SIX MONTHS LATER...
RF

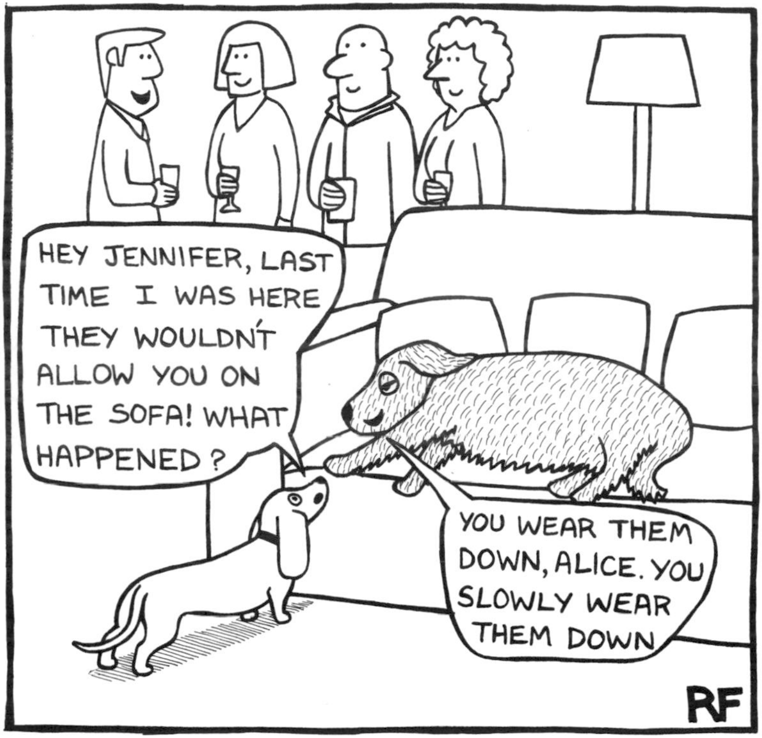
HEY JENNIFER, LAST TIME I WAS HERE THEY WOULDN'T ALLOW YOU ON THE SOFA! WHAT HAPPENED?
YOU WEAR THEM DOWN, ALICE. YOU SLOWLY WEAR THEM DOWN
RF

THINGS DOGS ARE NOT VERY GOOD AT No.3...

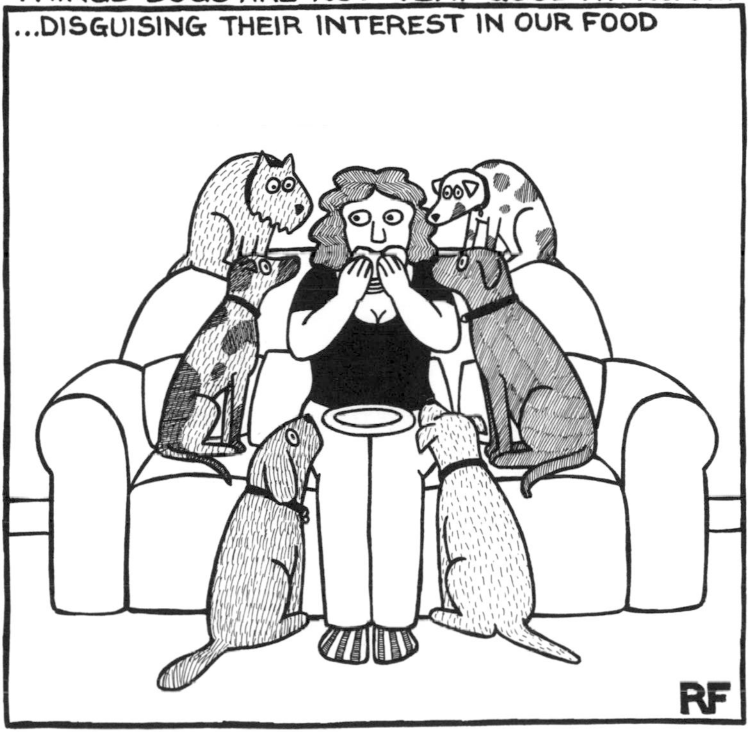
...DISGUISING THEIR INTEREST IN OUR FOOD
RF

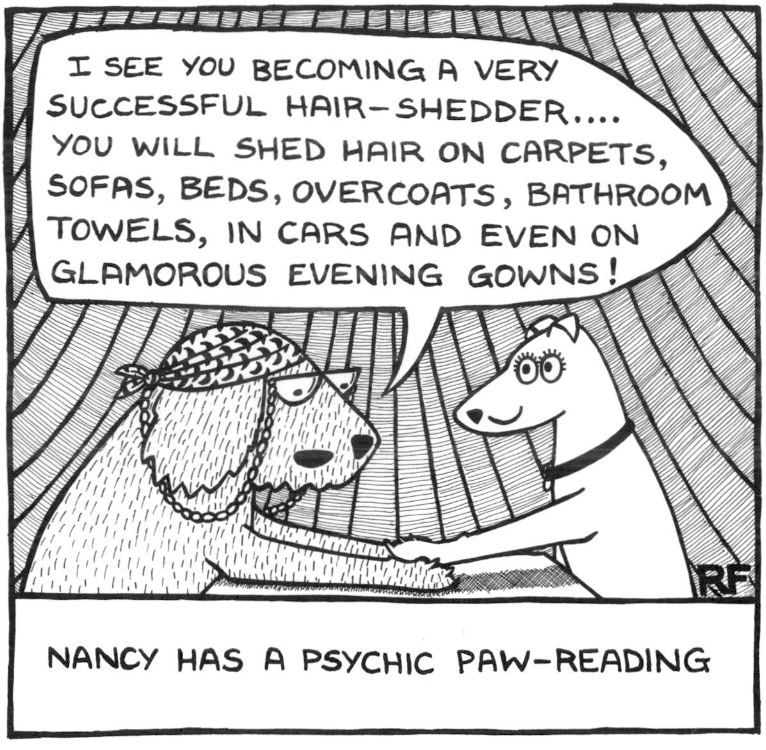
I SEE YOU BECOMING A VERY SUCCESSFUL HAIR-SHEDDER.... YOU WILL SHED HAIR ON CARPETS, SOFAS, BEDS, OVERCOATS, BATHROOM TOWELS, IN CARS AND EVEN ON GLAMOROUS EVENING GOWNS!
RF

NANCY HAS A PSYCHIC PAW-READING

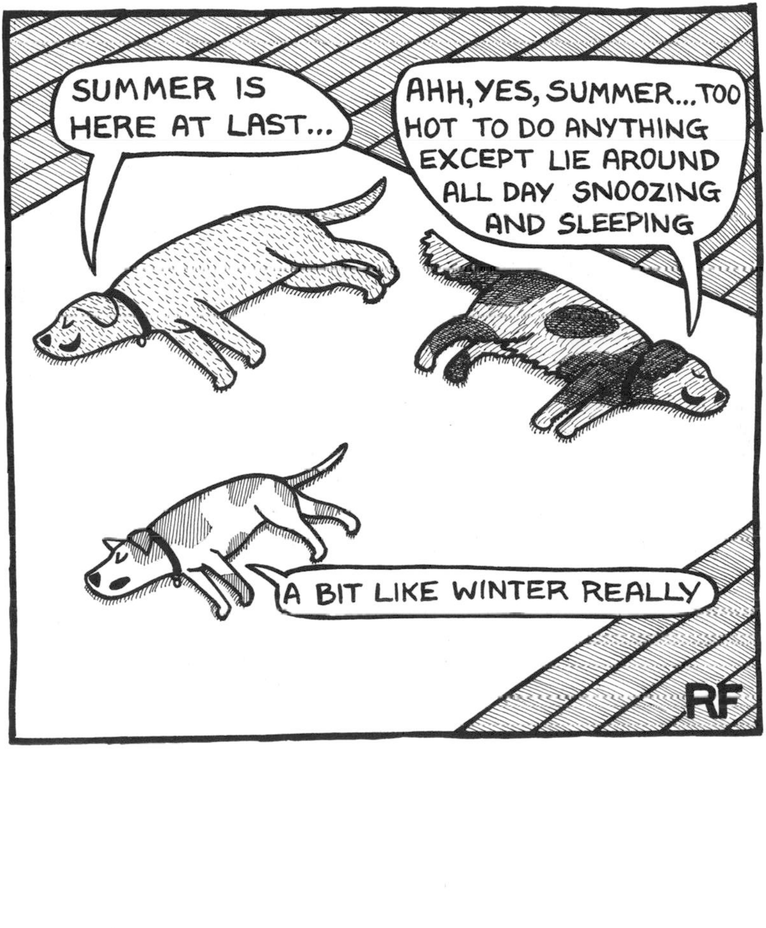
SUMMER IS HERE AT LAST...
AHH, YES, SUMMER...TOO HOT TO DO ANYTHING EXCEPT LIE AROUND ALL DAY SNOOZING AND SLEEPING
A BIT LIKE WINTER REALLY
RF

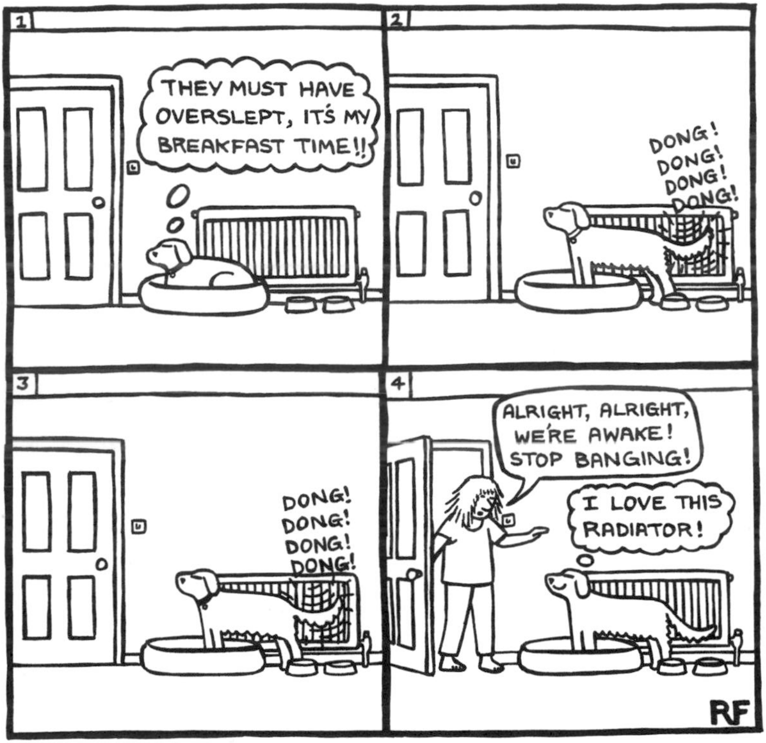
1
THEY MUST HAVE OVERSLEPT, IT'S MY BREAKFAST TIME!!
2
DONG! DONG! DONG! DONG!
3
DONG! DONG! DONG! DONG!
4
ALRIGHT, ALRIGHT, WE'RE AWAKE! STOP BANGING!
I LOVE THIS RADIATOR!
RF

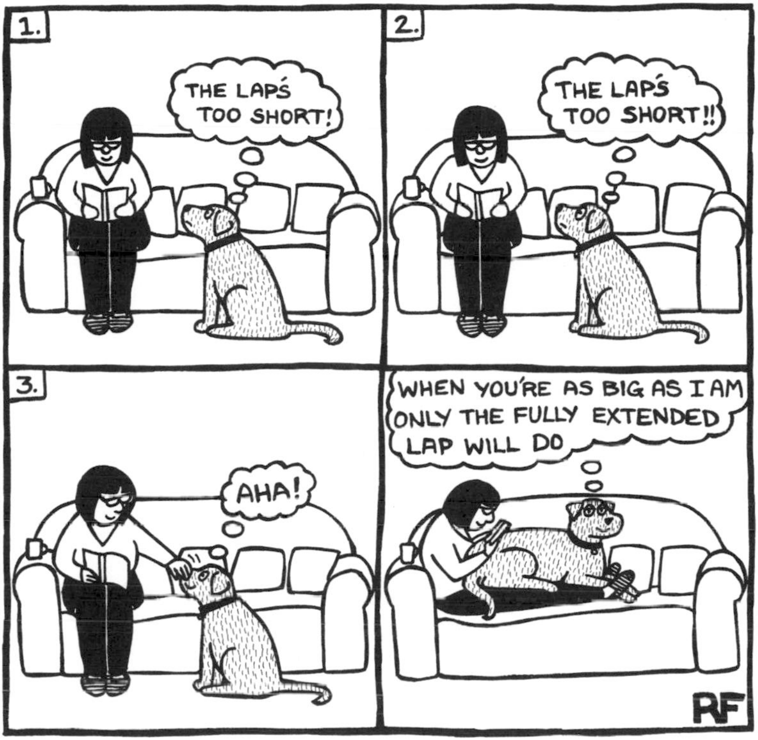
1.
THE LAP'S TOO SHORT!
2.
THE LAP'S TOO SHORT!!
3.
AHA!
WHEN YOU'RE AS BIG AS I AM ONLY THE FULLY EXTENDED LAP WILL DO
RF

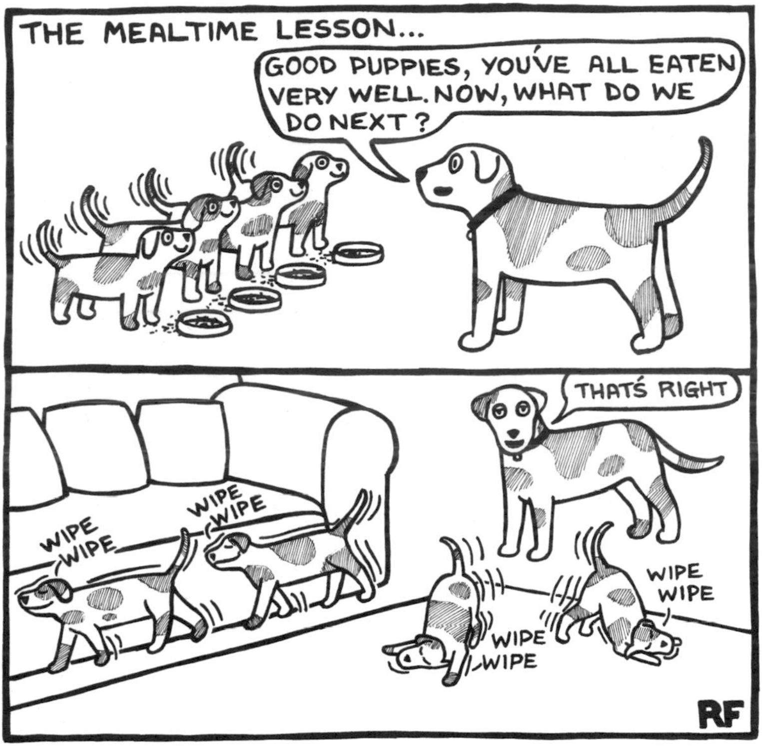
THE MEALTIME LESSON...
GOOD PUPPIES, YOU'VE ALL EATEN VERY WELL. NOW, WHAT DO WE DO NEXT?
WIPE WIPE
WIPE WIPE
THAT'S RIGHT
WIPE WIPE
WIPE WIPE
RF

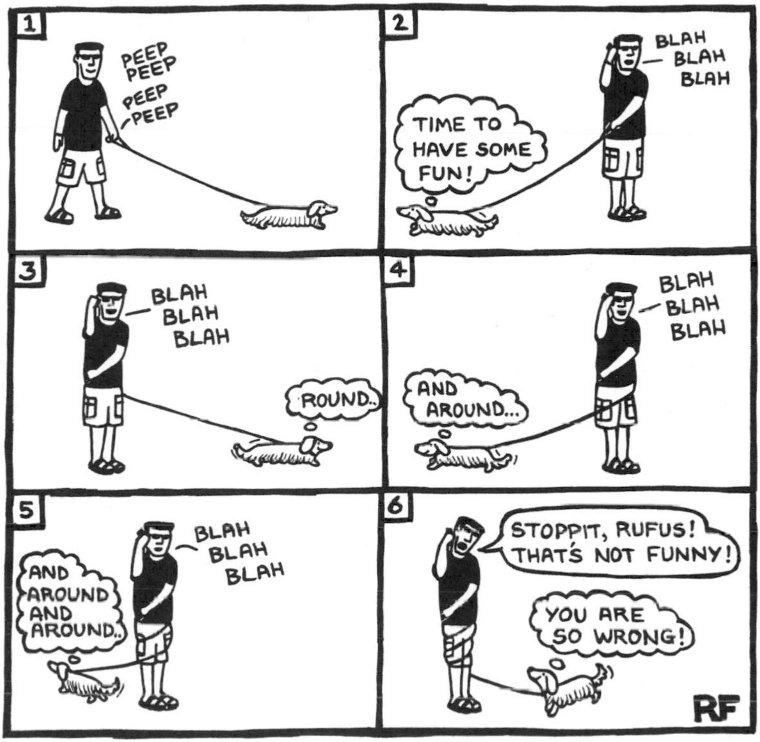
1
PEEP
PEEP
PEEP
PEEP
2
BLAH
BLAH
BLAH
TIME TO HAVE SOME FUN!
3
BLAH
BLAH
BLAH
ROUND..
4
BLAH
BLAH
BLAH
AND AROUND...
5
BLAH
BLAH
BLAH
AND AROUND AND AROUND..
6
STOPPIT, RUFUS! THAT'S NOT FUNNY!
YOU ARE SO WRONG!
RF

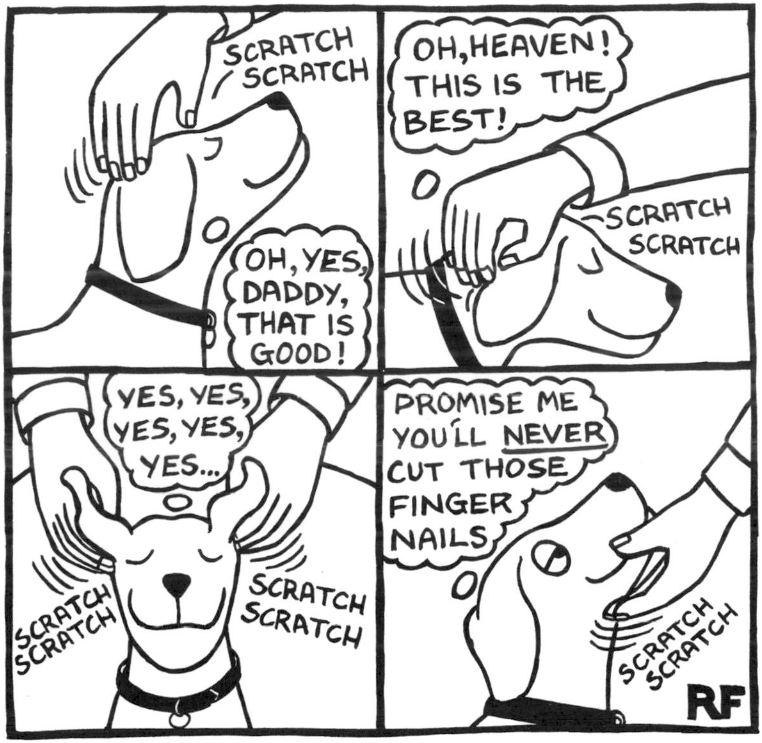
SCRATCH SCRATCH
OH, YES, DADDY, THAT IS GOOD!
OH, HEAVEN! THIS IS THE BEST!
SCRATCH SCRATCH
YES, YES, YES, YES, YES...
SCRATCH SCRATCH
SCRATCH SCRATCH
PROMISE ME YOU'LL NEVER CUT THOSE FINGER NAILS
SCRATCH SCRATCH
RF

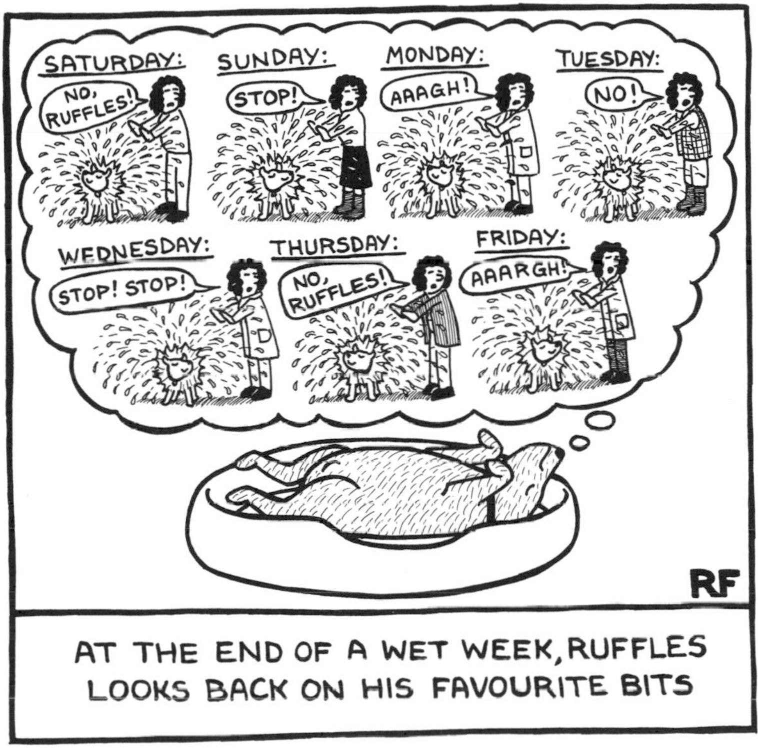
SATURDAY:
NO, RUFFLES!
SUNDAY:
STOP!
MONDAY:
AAAGH!
TUESDAY:
NO!
WEDNESDAY:
STOP! STOP!
THURSDAY:
NO, RUFFLES!
FRIDAY:
AAARGH!
RF

AT THE END OF A WET WEEK, RUFFLES LOOKS BACK ON HIS FAVOURITE BITS

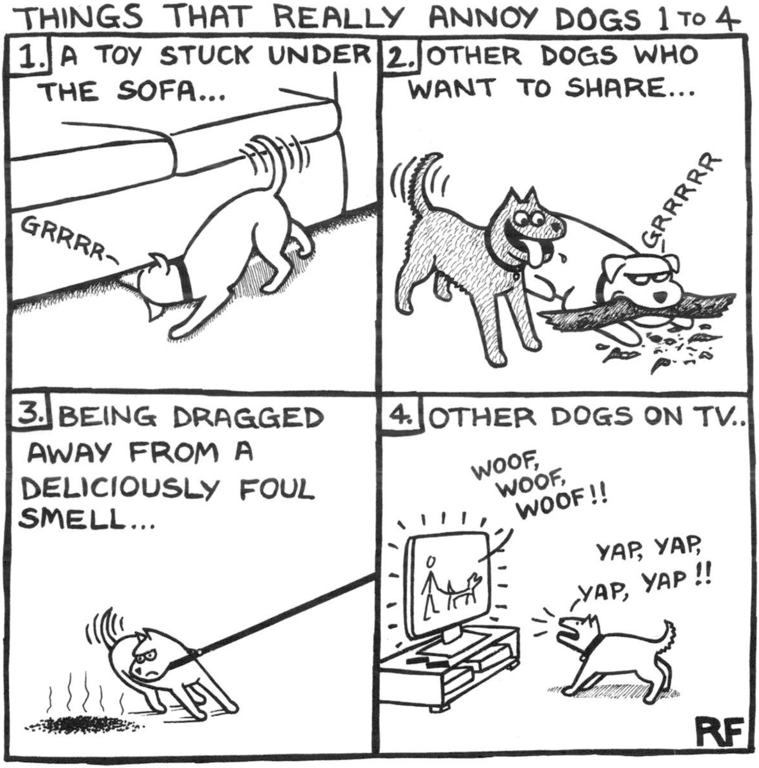
THINGS THAT REALLY ANNOY DOGS 1 TO 4
1. A TOY STUCK UNDER THE SOFA...
GRRRRR
2. OTHER DOGS WHO WANT TO SHARE...
GRRRRRR
3. BEING DRAGGED AWAY FROM A DELICIOUSLY FOUL SMELL...
4. OTHER DOGS ON TV..
WOOF, WOOF, WOOF!!
YAP, YAP, YAP, YAP!!
RF

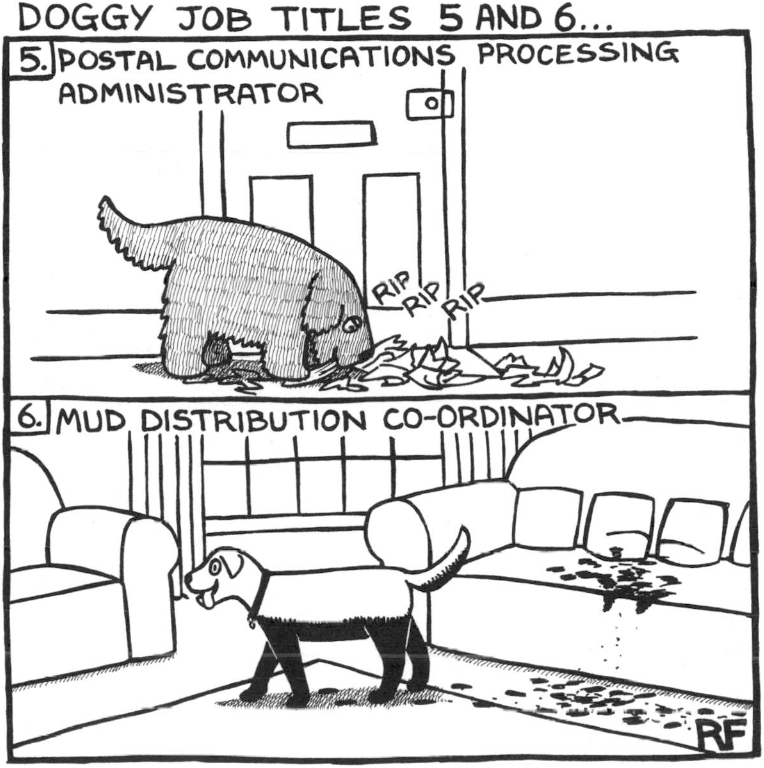
DOGGY JOB TITLES 5 AND 6...
5. POSTAL COMMUNICATIONS PROCESSING ADMINISTRATOR
RIP
RIP
RIP
6. MUD DISTRIBUTION CO-ORDINATOR
RF

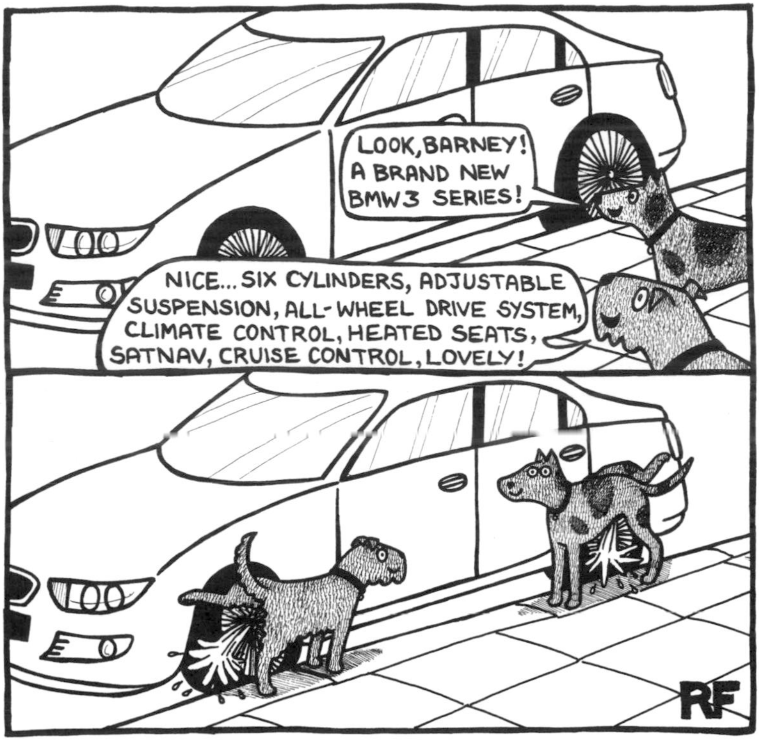
LOOK, BARNEY! A BRAND NEW BMW3 SERIES!
NICE... SIX CYLINDERS, ADJUSTABLE SUSPENSION, ALL-WHEEL DRIVE SYSTEM, CLIMATE CONTROL, HEATED SEATS, SATNAV, CRUISE CONTROL, LOVELY!
RF

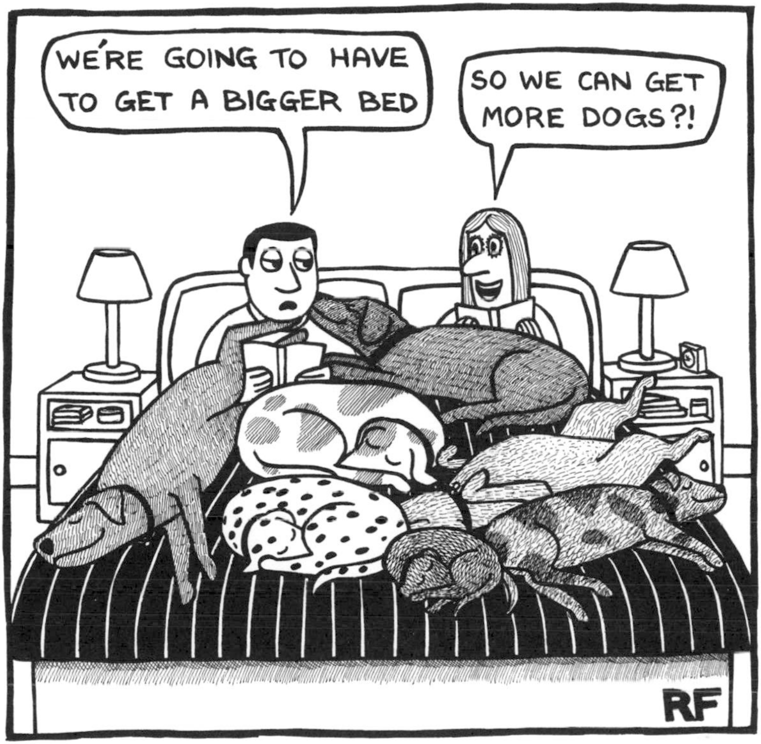
WE'RE GOING TO HAVE TO GET A BIGGER BED
SO WE CAN GET MORE DOGS?!
RF

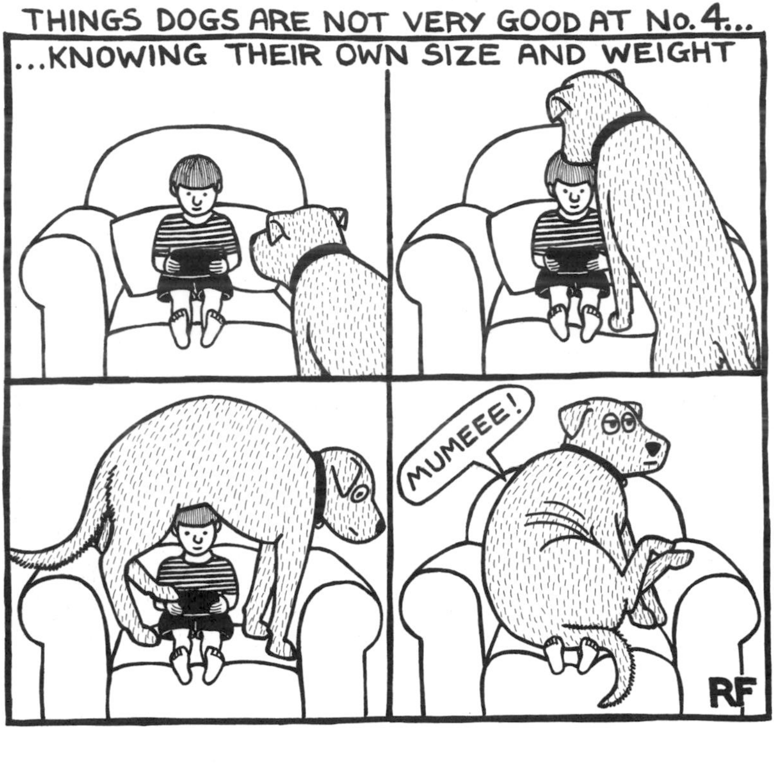
THINGS DOGS ARE NOT VERY GOOD AT No. 4...
...KNOWING THEIR OWN SIZE AND WEIGHT
MUMEEE!
RF

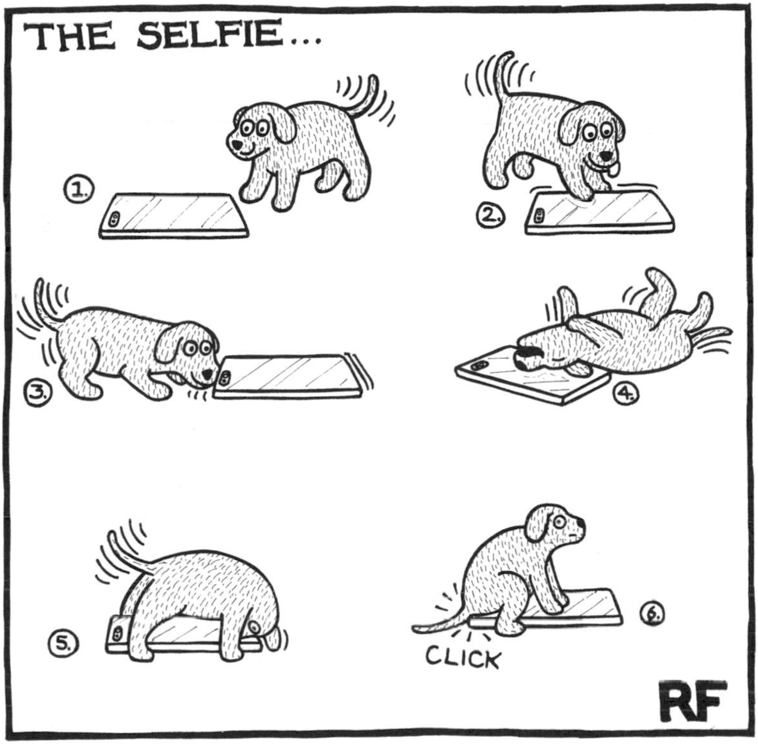
THE SELFIE...
1.
2.
3.
4.
5.
6.
CLICK
RF

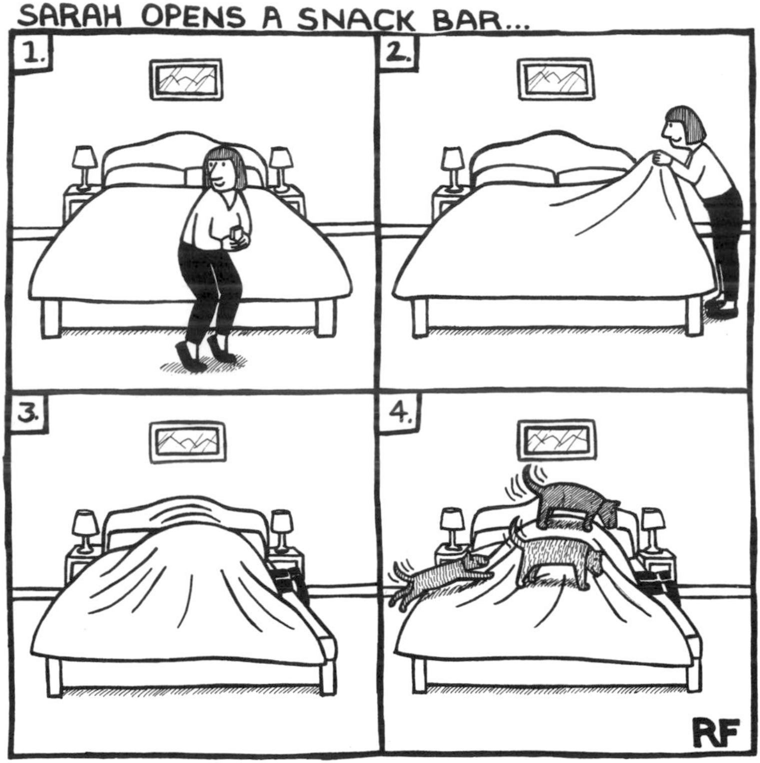
SARAH OPENS A SNACK BAR...
1.
2.
3.
4.
RF

1.
I AM ABOUT TO GO INTO BATTLE...
2.
..THE DEVIL MONSTER HAS BEEN RELEASED FROM IT'S CAVE! I CAN HEAR IT COMING!...
3.
..IT WANTS TO DEVOUR ME, BUT I WILL NOT BE DEVOURED! I WILL FIGHT! I WILL BITE! I WILL DESTROY THE EVIL BEAST! HERE IT COMES!!...
4.
YAP YAP YAP YAP
DIE BEAST, DIE!
RF

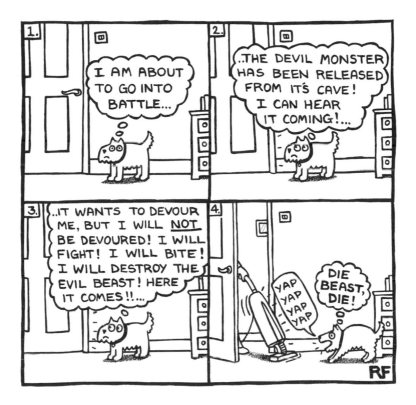

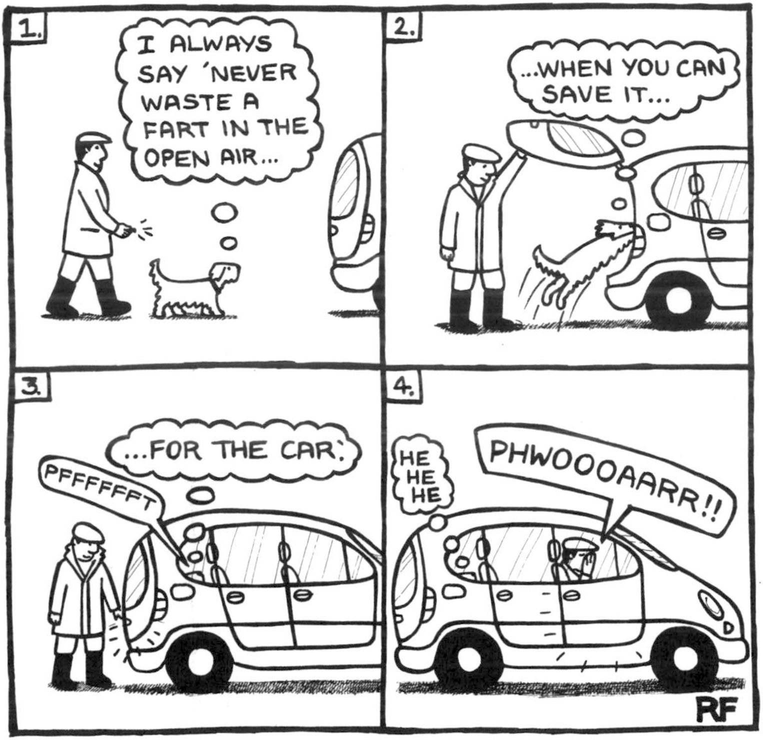
1.
I ALWAYS SAY 'NEVER WASTE A FART IN THE OPEN AIR...
2.
...WHEN YOU CAN SAVE IT...
3.
...FOR THE CAR.'
PFFFFFFT
4.
HE HE HE
PHWOOOOAARR!!
RF

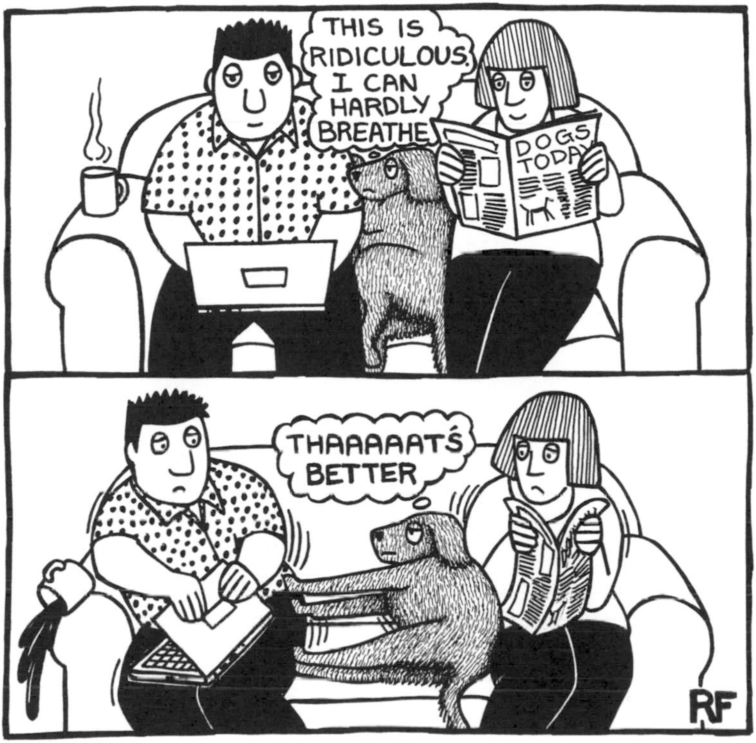
THIS IS RIDICULOUS. I CAN HARDLY BREATHE
DOGS TODAY
THAAAAAT'S BETTER
RF

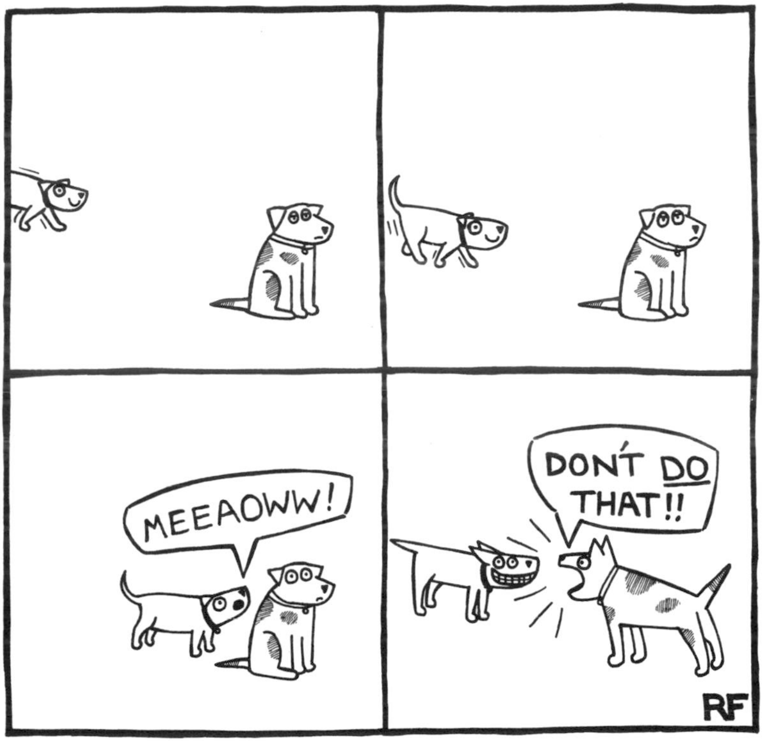
MEEAOWW!
DON'T DO THAT!!
RF

AT PUPPY SCHOOL...

1. A FEW MINUTES INTO THE JOURNEY START PANTING.

2. WIPE NOSES AND SALIVA ON WINDOWS.

3. WHIMPER EXCITEDLY.

4. AS CAR GETS CLOSER TO PARK YELP LOUDLY AND LEAP ABOUT.

5. AS SOON AS YOU GET OUT OF CAR PEE IMMEDIATELY.

MR LEIBOWITZ SUMMARISES HIS CAR JOURNEYS LESSON WITH A FEW BULLET POINTS

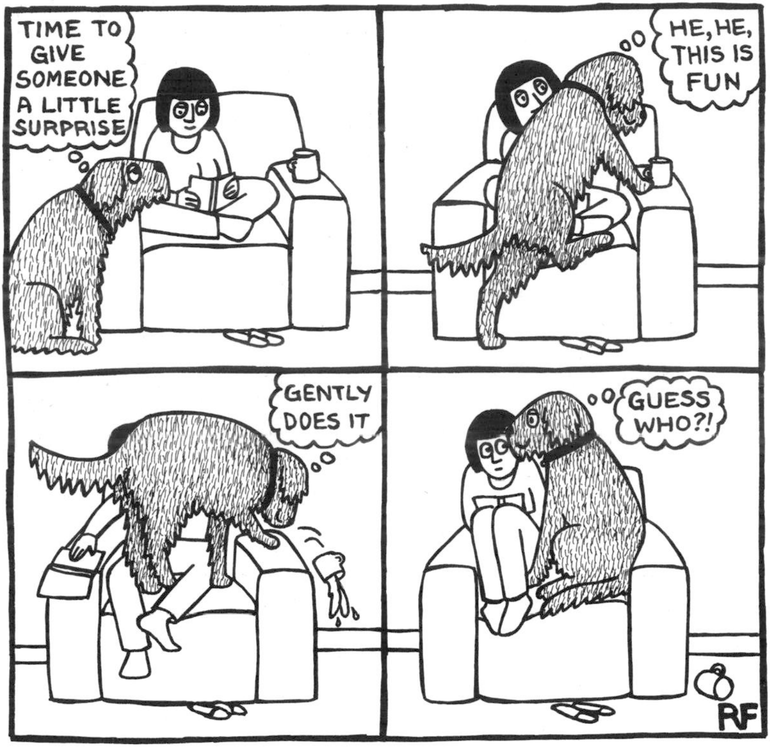
TIME TO GIVE SOMEONE A LITTLE SURPRISE
HE, HE, THIS IS FUN
GENTLY DOES IT
GUESS WHO?!
RF

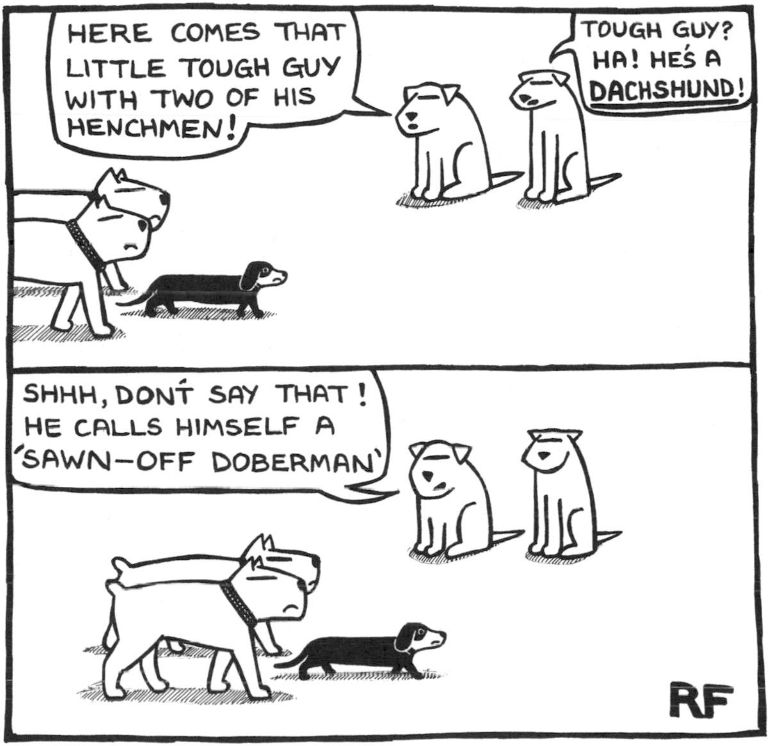
HERE COMES THAT LITTLE TOUGH GUY WITH TWO OF HIS HENCHMEN!
TOUGH GUY? HA! HE'S A DACHSHUND!
SHHH, DON'T SAY THAT! HE CALLS HIMSELF A 'SAWN-OFF DOBERMAN'
RF

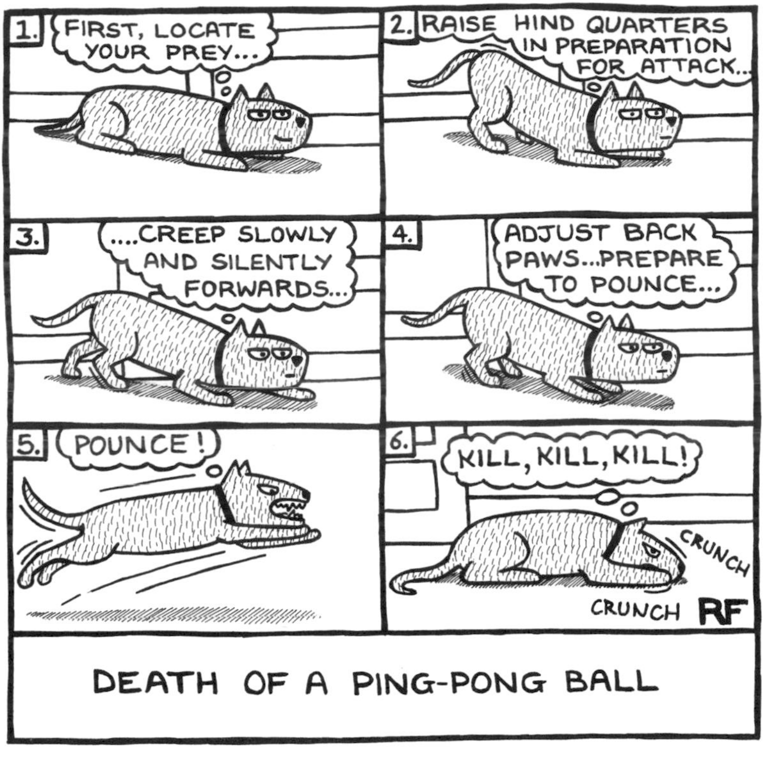
1.
FIRST, LOCATE YOUR PREY...
2.
RAISE HIND QUARTERS IN PREPARATION FOR ATTACK...
3.
....CREEP SLOWLY AND SILENTLY FORWARDS...
4.
ADJUST BACK PAWS...PREPARE TO POUNCE...
5.
POUNCE!
6.
KILL, KILL, KILL!
CRUNCH
CRUNCH
RF

DEATH OF A PING-PONG BALL

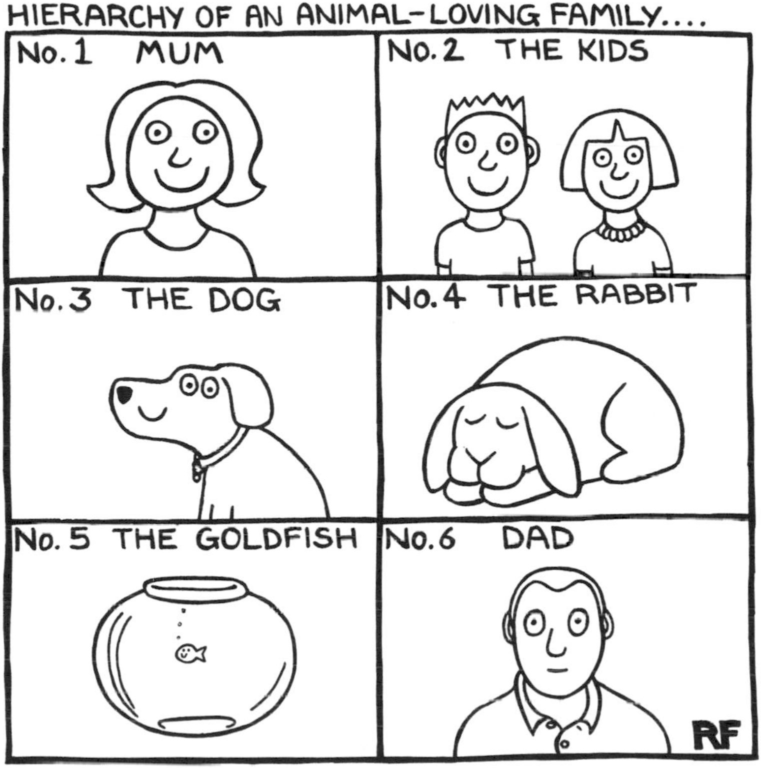
HIERARCHY OF AN ANIMAL-LOVING FAMILY....
No. 1 MUM
No. 2 THE KIDS
No. 3 THE DOG
No. 4 THE RABBIT
No. 5 THE GOLDFISH
No. 6 DAD
RF

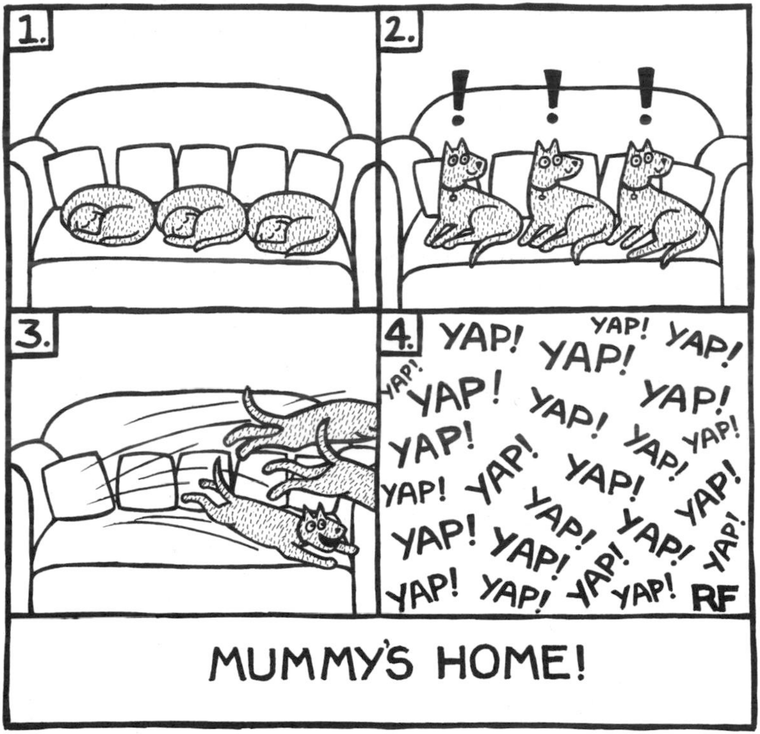
1.
2.
! ! !
3.
4.
YAP! YAP! YAP! YAP!
YAP! YAP! YAP! YAP!
YAP! YAP! YAP! YAP!
YAP! YAP! YAP! YAP!
YAP! YAP! YAP! YAP!
YAP! YAP! YAP! YAP! YAP!
RF
MUMMY'S HOME!

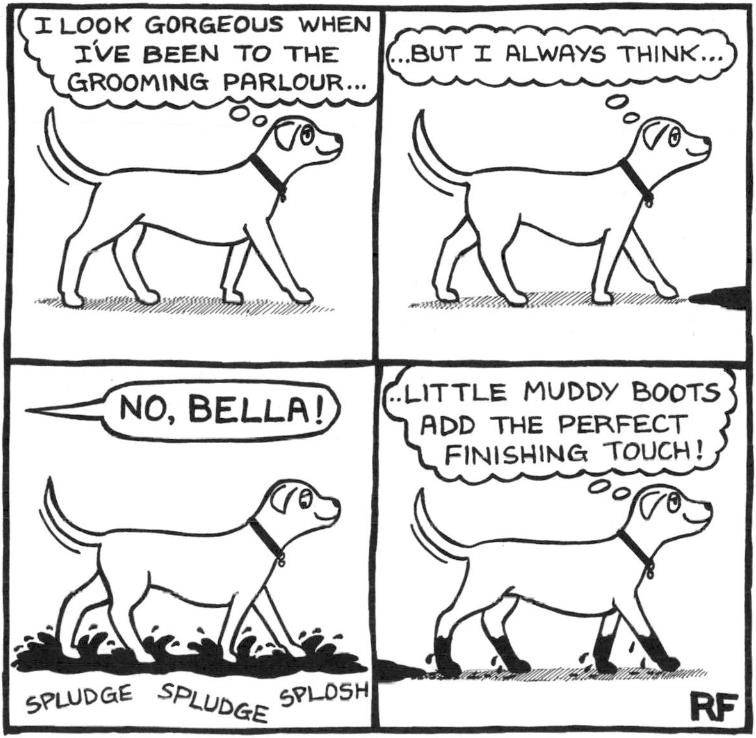
I LOOK GORGEOUS WHEN I'VE BEEN TO THE GROOMING PARLOUR...
...BUT I ALWAYS THINK...
NO, BELLA!
SPLUDGE SPLUDGE SPLOSH
..LITTLE MUDDY BOOTS ADD THE PERFECT FINISHING TOUCH!
RF

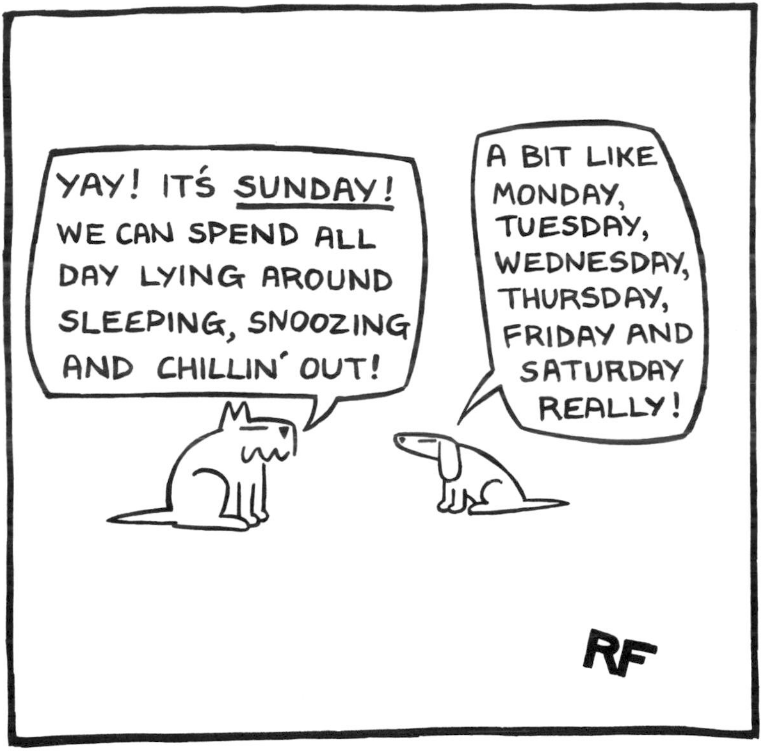
YAY! IT'S SUNDAY! WE CAN SPEND ALL DAY LYING AROUND SLEEPING, SNOOZING AND CHILLIN' OUT!
A BIT LIKE MONDAY, TUESDAY, WEDNESDAY, THURSDAY, FRIDAY AND SATURDAY REALLY!
RF

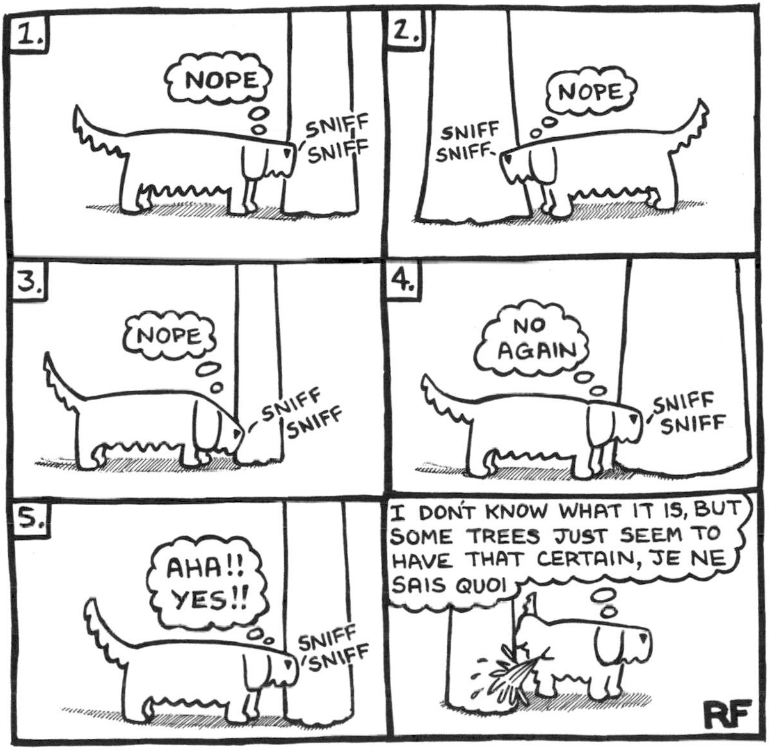
1.
NOPE
SNIFF SNIFF
2.
NOPE
SNIFF SNIFF
3.
NOPE
SNIFF SNIFF
4.
NO AGAIN
SNIFF SNIFF
5.
AHA!! YES!!
SNIFF SNIFF
I DON'T KNOW WHAT IT IS, BUT SOME TREES JUST SEEM TO HAVE THAT CERTAIN, JE NE SAIS QUOI
RF

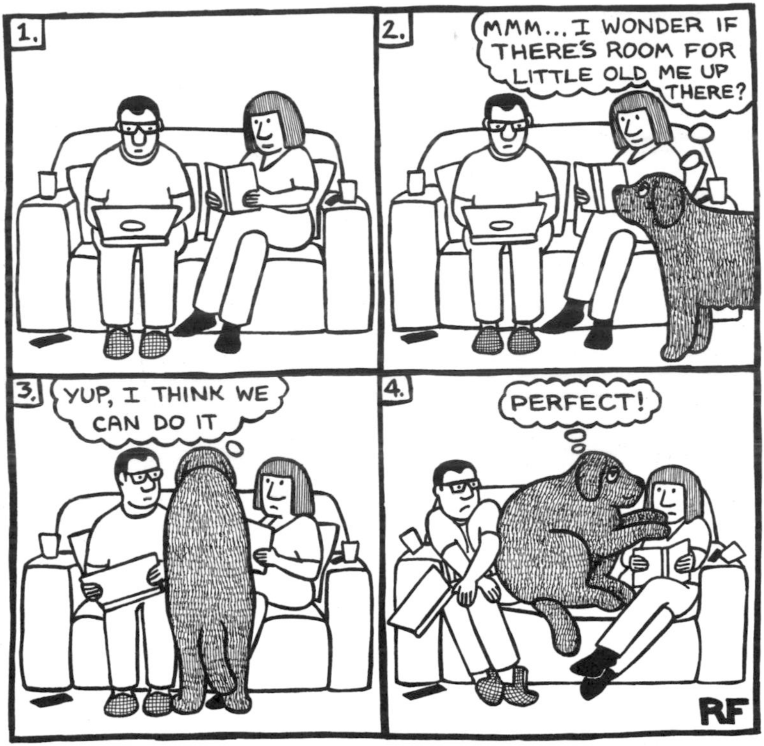
1.
2.
MMM... I WONDER IF THERE'S ROOM FOR LITTLE OLD ME UP THERE?
3.
YUP, I THINK WE CAN DO IT
4.
PERFECT!
RF

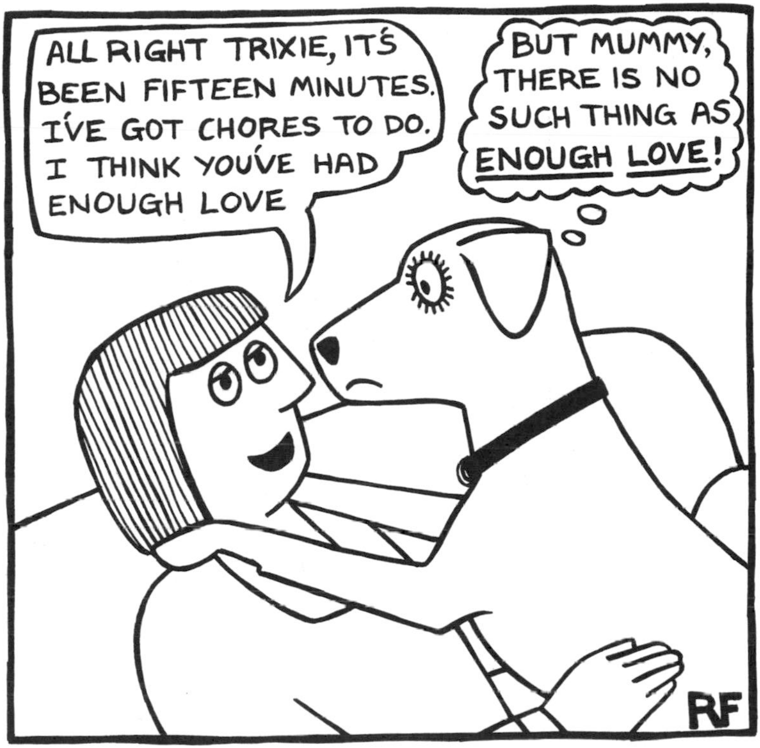
ALL RIGHT TRIXIE, IT'S BEEN FIFTEEN MINUTES. I'VE GOT CHORES TO DO. I THINK YOU'VE HAD ENOUGH LOVE
BUT MUMMY, THERE IS NO SUCH THING AS ENOUGH LOVE!
RF

FAMOUS DOG MOTTOS...

"SHARE YOUR MUD WITH
THE ONES YOU LOVE"

RF

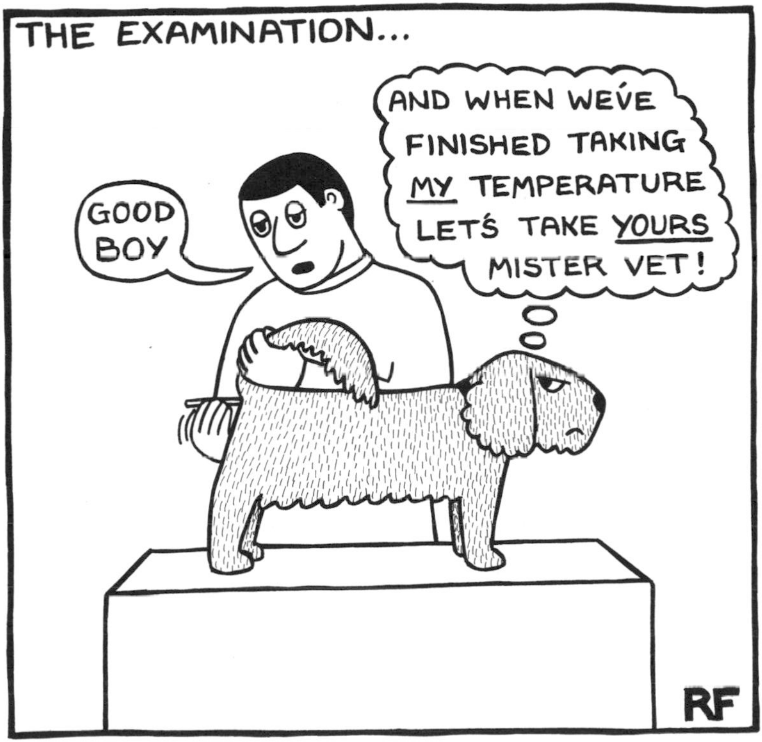
THE EXAMINATION...
GOOD BOY
AND WHEN WEVE FINISHED TAKING MY TEMPERATURE LETS TAKE YOURS MISTER VET!
RF

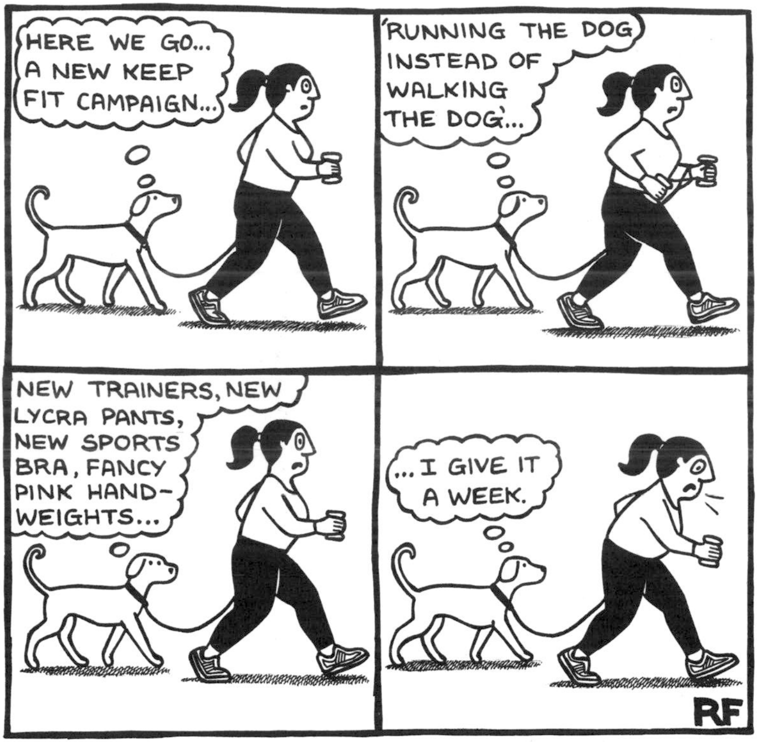
HERE WE GO... A NEW KEEP FIT CAMPAIGN...
'RUNNING THE DOG INSTEAD OF WALKING THE DOG'...
NEW TRAINERS, NEW LYCRA PANTS, NEW SPORTS BRA, FANCY PINK HAND-WEIGHTS...
...I GIVE IT A WEEK.
RF

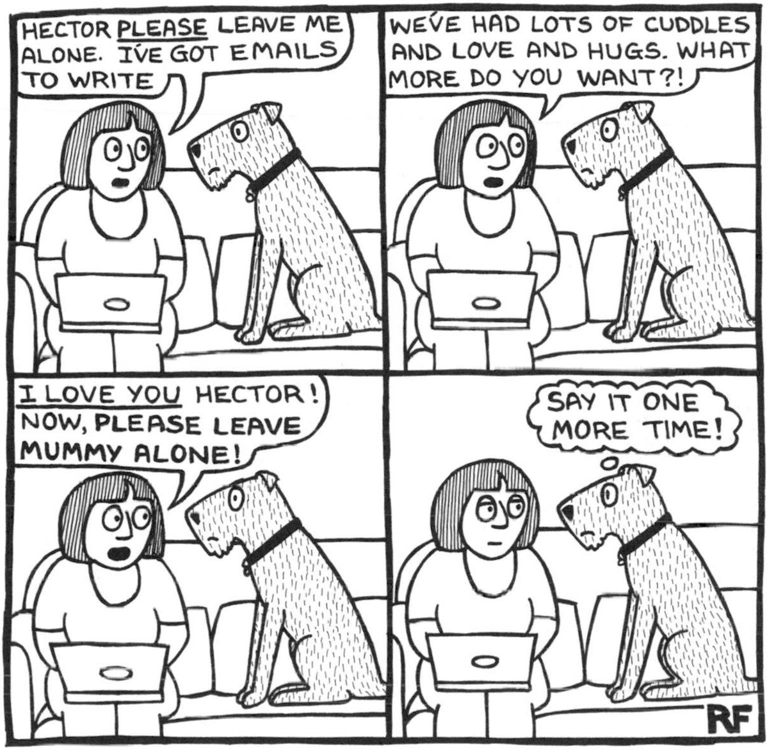
HECTOR PLEASE LEAVE ME ALONE. I'VE GOT EMAILS TO WRITE
WE'VE HAD LOTS OF CUDDLES AND LOVE AND HUGS. WHAT MORE DO YOU WANT?!
I LOVE YOU HECTOR! NOW, PLEASE LEAVE MUMMY ALONE!
SAY IT ONE MORE TIME!
RF

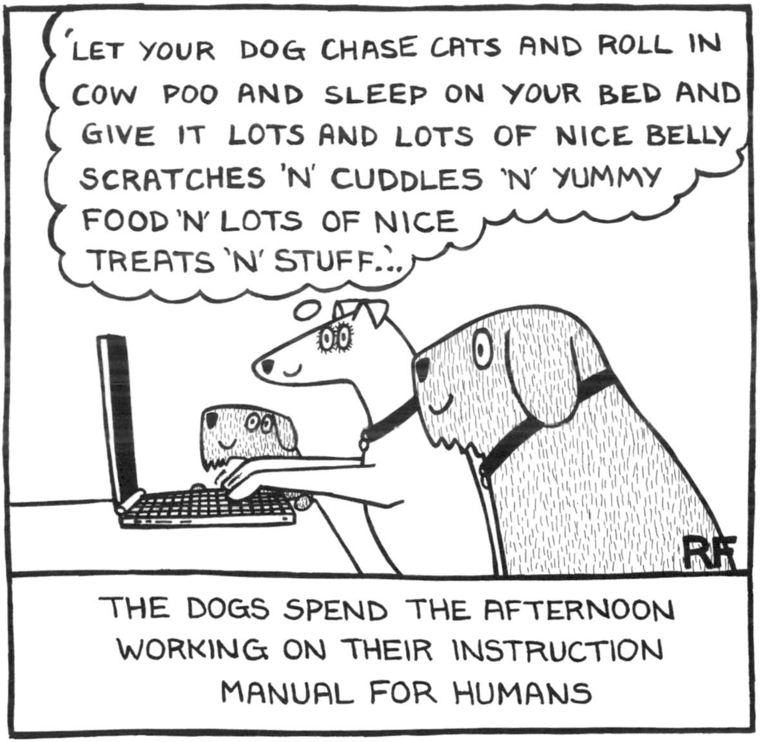
'LET YOUR DOG CHASE CATS AND ROLL IN COW POO AND SLEEP ON YOUR BED AND GIVE IT LOTS AND LOTS OF NICE BELLY SCRATCHES 'N' CUDDLES 'N' YUMMY FOOD 'N' LOTS OF NICE TREATS 'N' STUFF...'
RF
THE DOGS SPEND THE AFTERNOON WORKING ON THEIR INSTRUCTION MANUAL FOR HUMANS

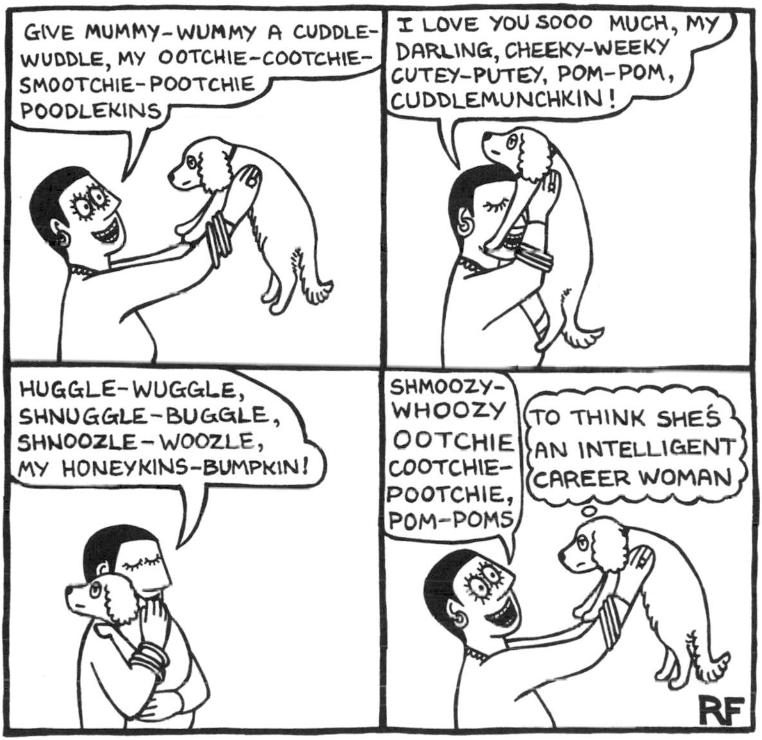
GIVE MUMMY-WUMMY A CUDDLE-WUDDLE, MY OOTCHIE-COOTCHIE-SMOOTCHIE-POOTCHIE POODLEKINS
I LOVE YOU SOOO MUCH, MY DARLING, CHEEKY-WEEKY CUTEY-PUTEY, POM-POM, CUDDLEMUNCHKIN!
HUGGLE-WUGGLE, SHNUGGLE-BUGGLE, SHNOOZLE-WOOZLE, MY HONEYKINS-BUMPKIN!
SHMOOZY-WHOOZY OOTCHIE COOTCHIE-POOTCHIE, POM-POMS
TO THINK SHE'S AN INTELLIGENT CAREER WOMAN
RF

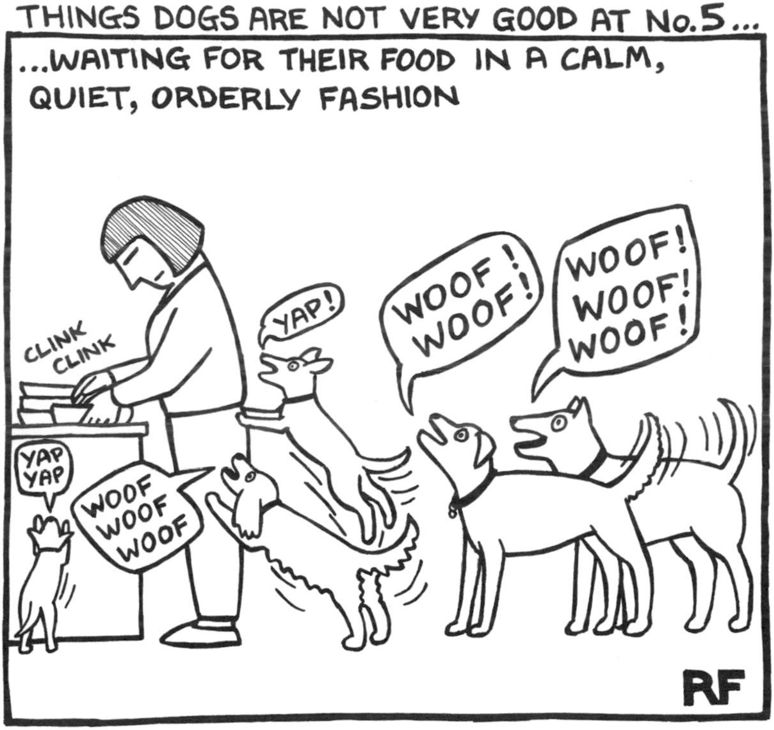
THINGS DOGS ARE NOT VERY GOOD AT No.5...
...WAITING FOR THEIR FOOD IN A CALM, QUIET, ORDERLY FASHION
CLINK CLINK
YAP YAP
WOOF WOOF WOOF
YAP!
WOOF! WOOF!
WOOF! WOOF! WOOF!
RF

DOGGY FACTS...

DOGS ARE HIGHLY SOCIAL ANIMALS WHO LIKE TO BE INVOLVED IN WHATEVER THEIR OWNER IS DOING...

RF

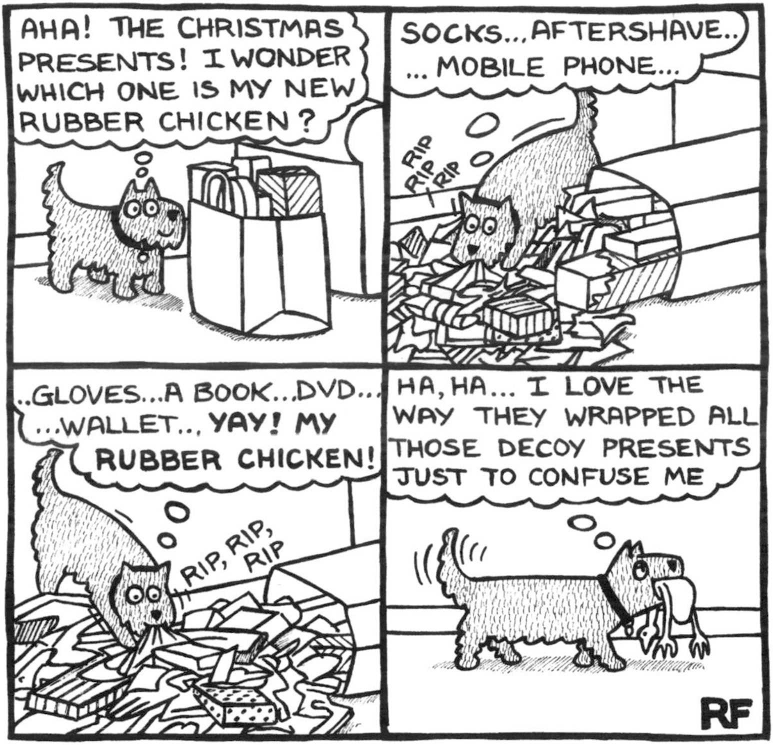
AHA! THE CHRISTMAS PRESENTS! I WONDER WHICH ONE IS MY NEW RUBBER CHICKEN?
SOCKS..., AFTERSHAVE.. ...MOBILE PHONE...
RIP RIP RIP
..GLOVES...A BOOK...DVD... ...WALLET.., YAY! MY RUBBER CHICKEN!
RIP, RIP, RIP
HA, HA... I LOVE THE WAY THEY WRAPPED ALL THOSE DECOY PRESENTS JUST TO CONFUSE ME
RF

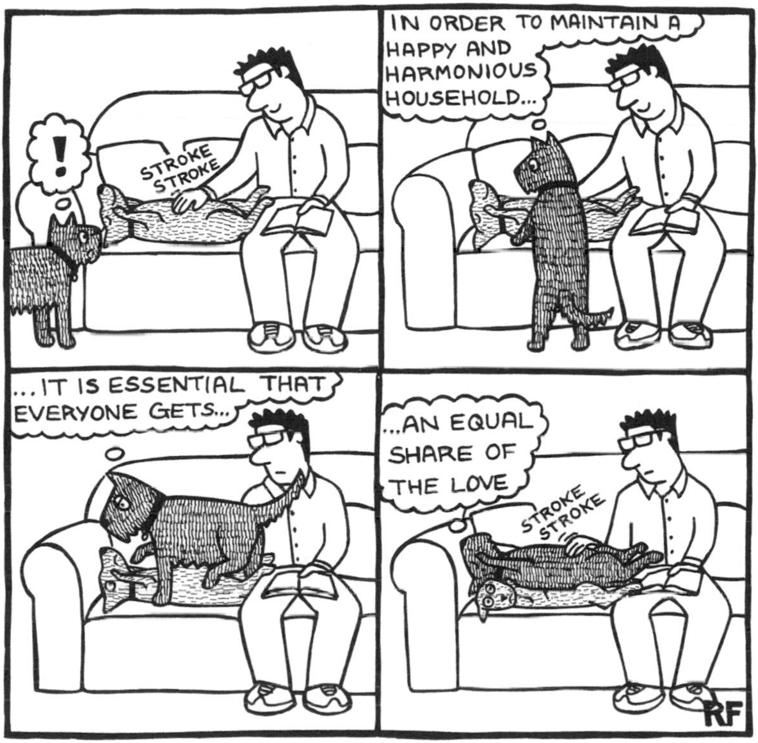
!
STROKE STROKE
IN ORDER TO MAINTAIN A HAPPY AND HARMONIOUS HOUSEHOLD...
...IT IS ESSENTIAL THAT EVERYONE GETS...
...AN EQUAL SHARE OF THE LOVE
STROKE STROKE
RF

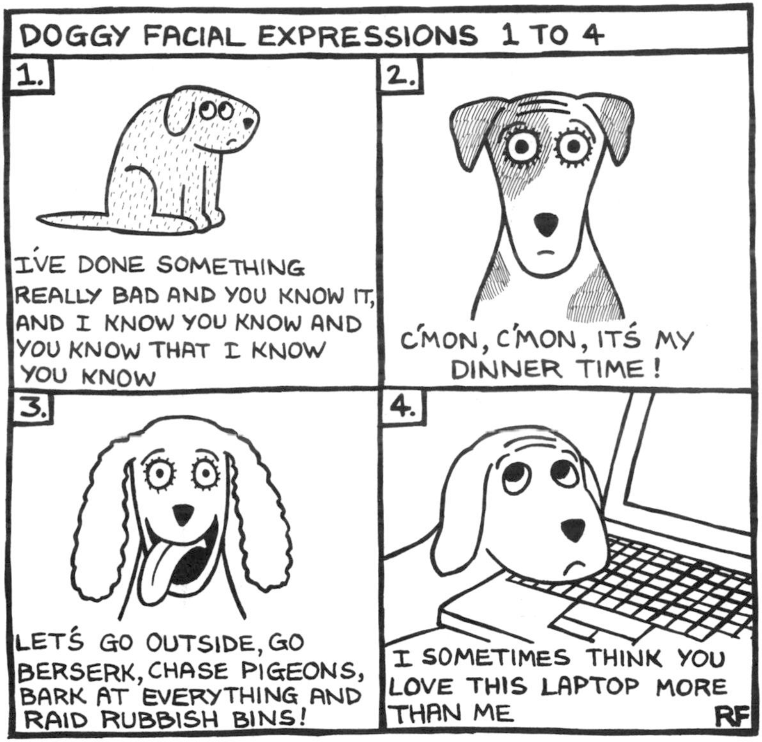
DOGGY FACIAL EXPRESSIONS 1 TO 4
1.
I'VE DONE SOMETHING REALLY BAD AND YOU KNOW IT, AND I KNOW YOU KNOW AND YOU KNOW THAT I KNOW YOU KNOW
2.
C'MON, C'MON, IT'S MY DINNER TIME!
3.
LET'S GO OUTSIDE, GO BERSERK, CHASE PIGEONS, BARK AT EVERYTHING AND RAID RUBBISH BINS!
4.
I SOMETIMES THINK YOU LOVE THIS LAPTOP MORE THAN ME
RF

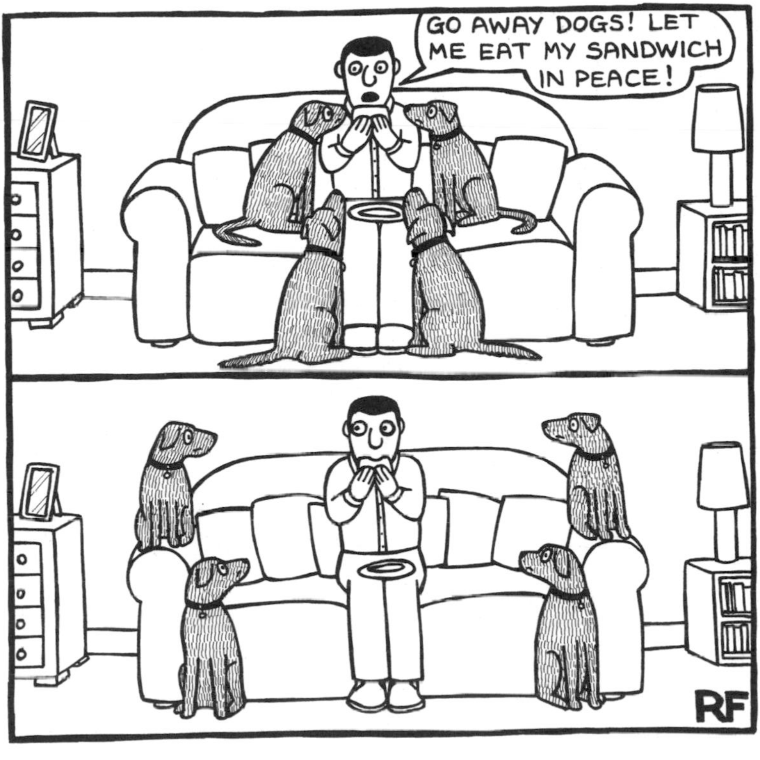
GO AWAY DOGS! LET ME EAT MY SANDWICH IN PEACE!
RF

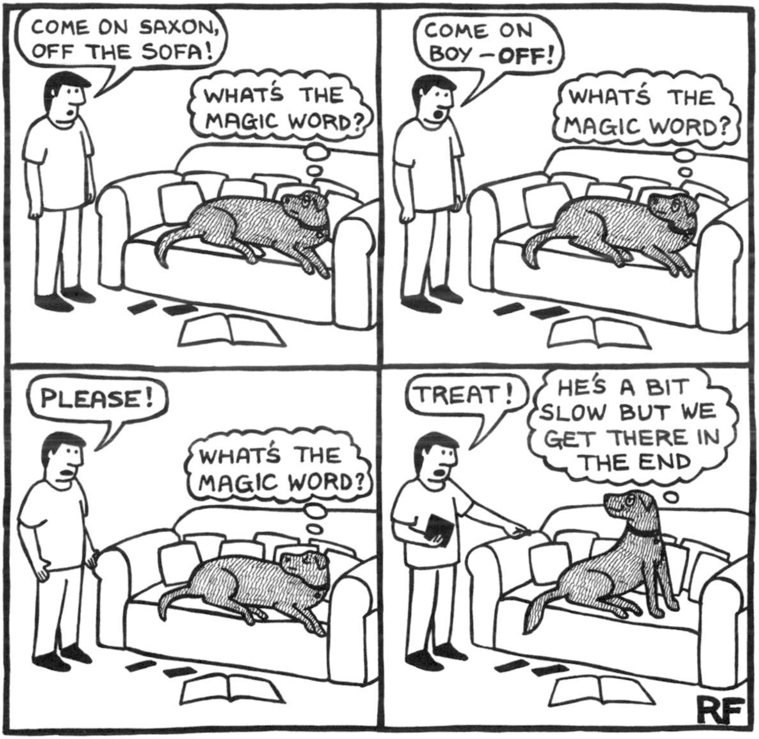
COME ON SAXON, OFF THE SOFA!
WHAT'S THE MAGIC WORD?
COME ON BOY – OFF!
WHAT'S THE MAGIC WORD?
PLEASE!
WHAT'S THE MAGIC WORD?
TREAT!
HE'S A BIT SLOW BUT WE GET THERE IN THE END
RF

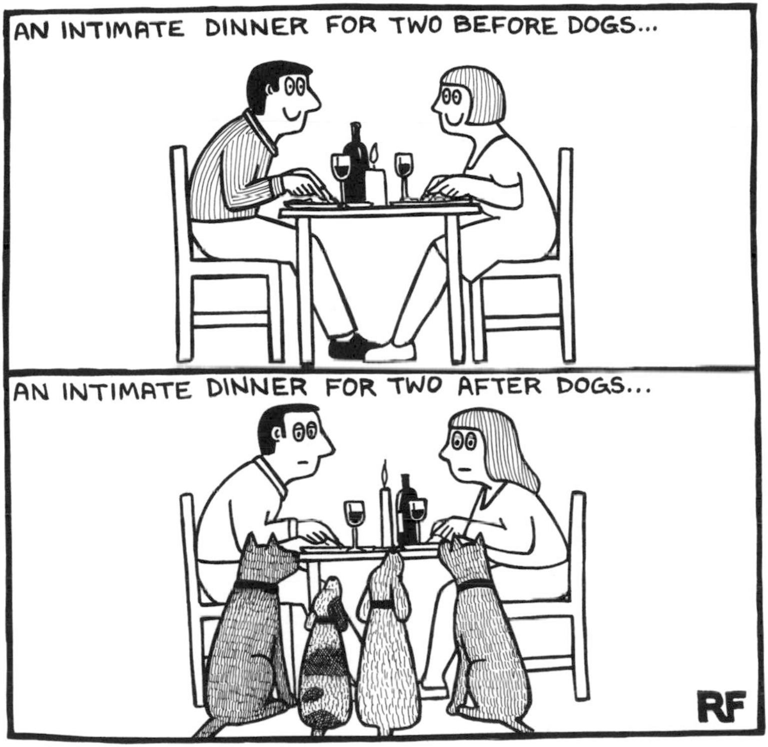
AN INTIMATE DINNER FOR TWO BEFORE DOGS...
AN INTIMATE DINNER FOR TWO AFTER DOGS...
RF

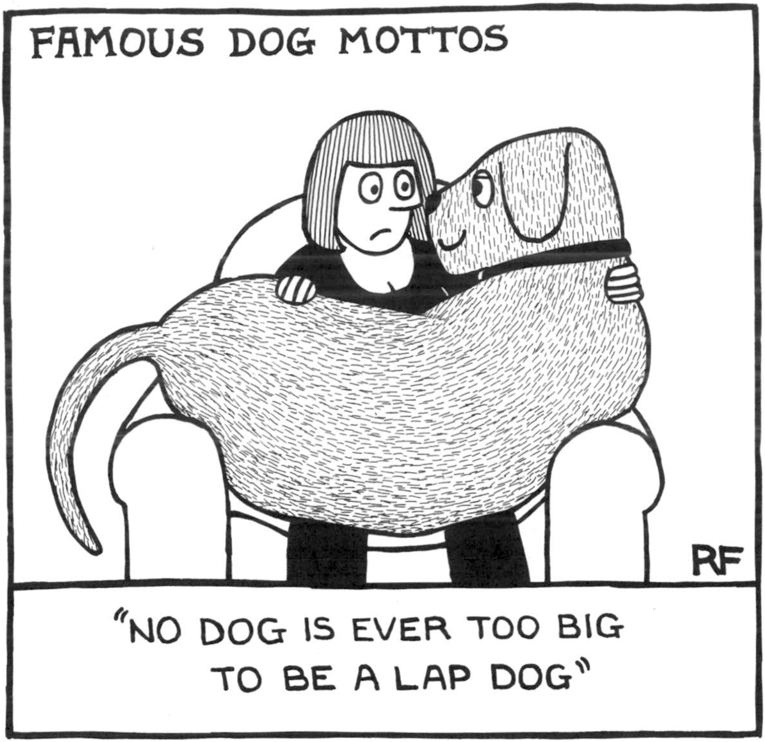
FAMOUS DOG MOTTOS
RF
"NO DOG IS EVER TOO BIG
TO BE A LAP DOG"

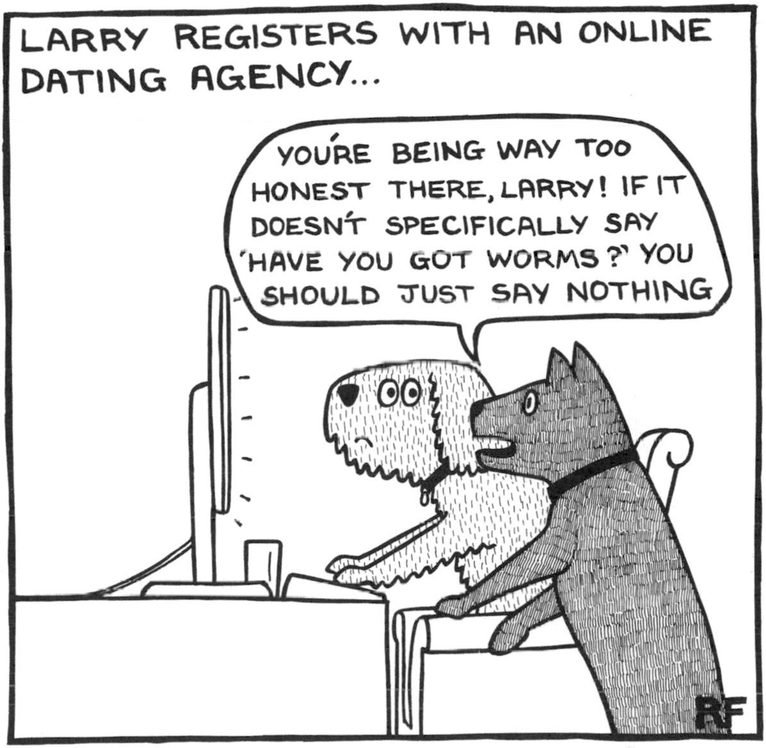
LARRY REGISTERS WITH AN ONLINE DATING AGENCY...
YOU'RE BEING WAY TOO HONEST THERE, LARRY! IF IT DOESN'T SPECIFICALLY SAY 'HAVE YOU GOT WORMS?' YOU SHOULD JUST SAY NOTHING
RF

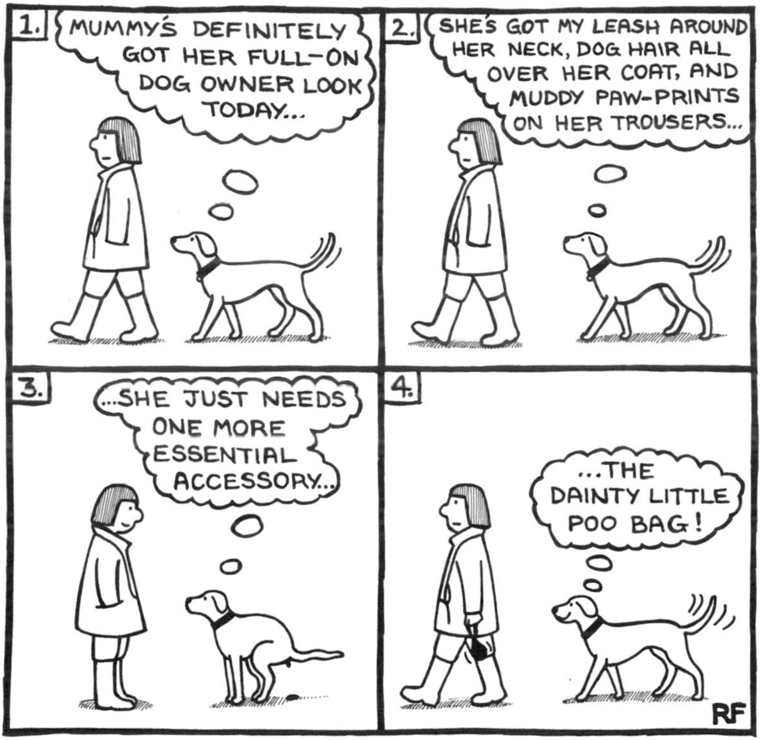
1.
MUMMY'S DEFINITELY GOT HER FULL-ON DOG OWNER LOOK TODAY...
2.
SHE'S GOT MY LEASH AROUND HER NECK, DOG HAIR ALL OVER HER COAT, AND MUDDY PAW-PRINTS ON HER TROUSERS...
3.
...SHE JUST NEEDS ONE MORE ESSENTIAL ACCESSORY...
4.
...THE DAINTY LITTLE POO BAG!
RF

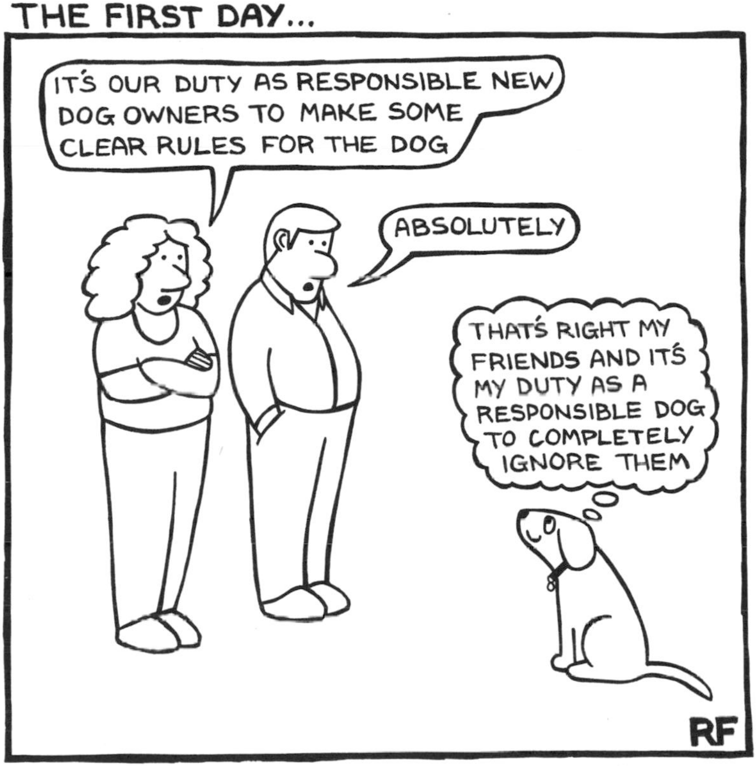
THE FIRST DAY...
IT'S OUR DUTY AS RESPONSIBLE NEW DOG OWNERS TO MAKE SOME CLEAR RULES FOR THE DOG
ABSOLUTELY
THAT'S RIGHT MY FRIENDS AND IT'S MY DUTY AS A RESPONSIBLE DOG TO COMPLETELY IGNORE THEM
RF

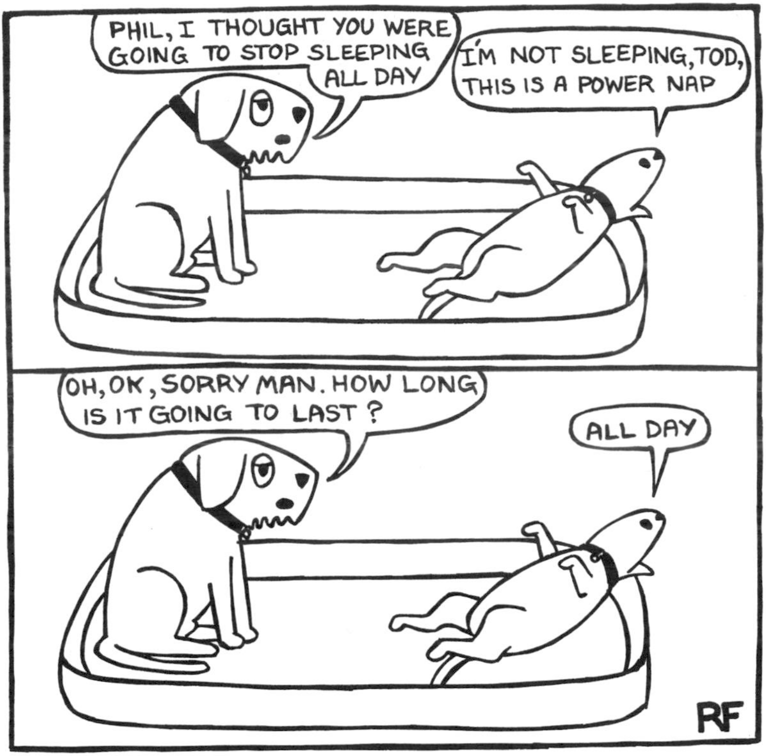
PHIL, I THOUGHT YOU WERE GOING TO STOP SLEEPING ALL DAY
I'M NOT SLEEPING, TOD, THIS IS A POWER NAP
OH, OK, SORRY MAN. HOW LONG IS IT GOING TO LAST ?
ALL DAY
RF

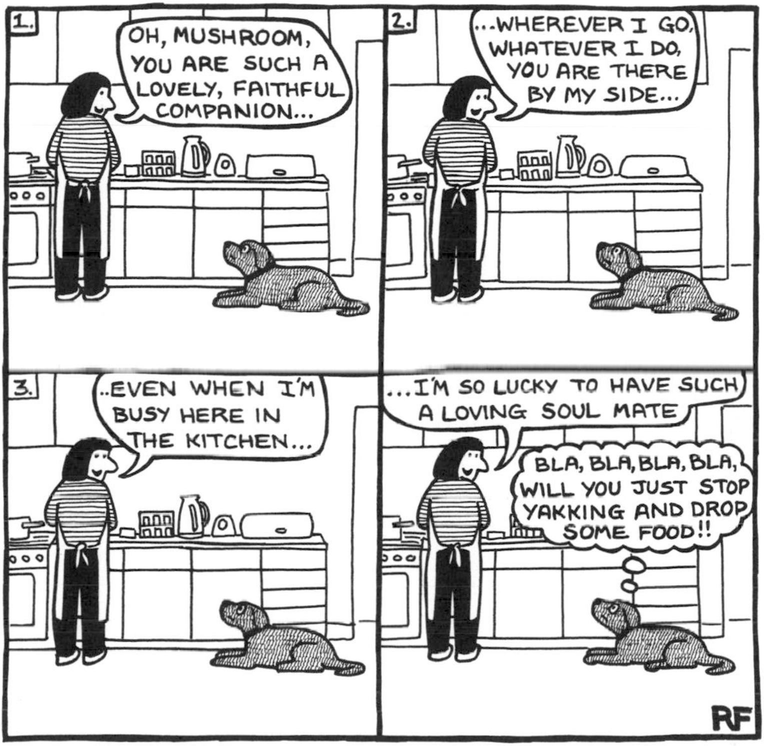
1.
OH, MUSHROOM, YOU ARE SUCH A LOVELY, FAITHFUL COMPANION...
2.
...WHEREVER I GO, WHATEVER I DO, YOU ARE THERE BY MY SIDE...
3.
..EVEN WHEN I'M BUSY HERE IN THE KITCHEN...
...I'M SO LUCKY TO HAVE SUCH A LOVING SOUL MATE
BLA, BLA, BLA, BLA, WILL YOU JUST STOP YAKKING AND DROP SOME FOOD!!
RF

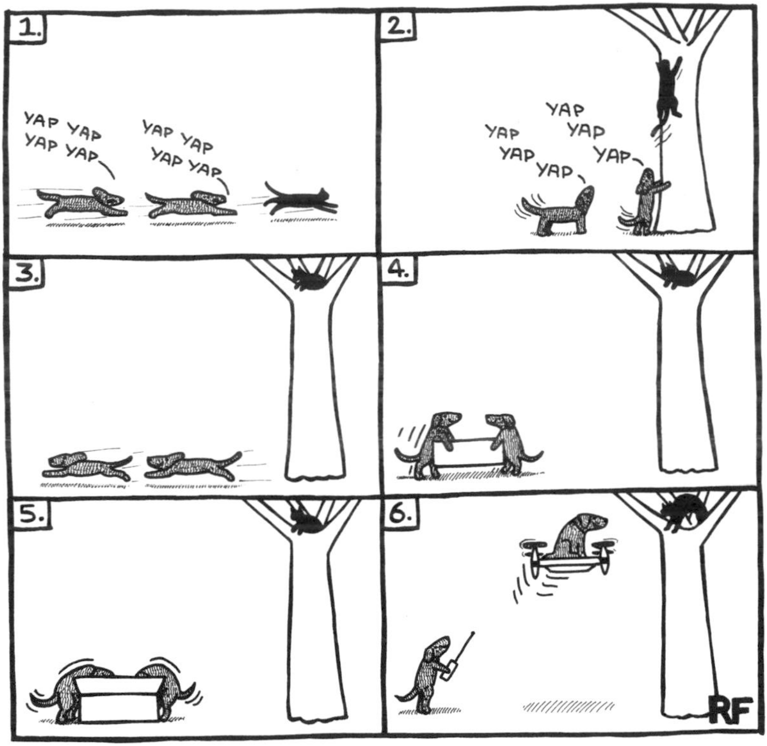
1.
YAP YAP
YAP YAP
YAP YAP
YAP YAP
2.
YAP
YAP
YAP
YAP
YAP
YAP
3.
4.
5.
6.
RF

AT PUPPY SCHOOL...
TODAY'S EXAM:
MEAL TIMES
..AND WHEN YOU'VE EATEN THE LAST MOUTHFUL WHAT DO YOU DO?
KEEP LICKING THE BOWL UNTIL IT REACHES THE OTHER SIDE OF THE ROOM, SIR!
RF

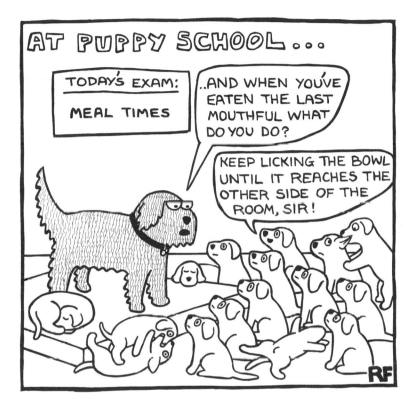

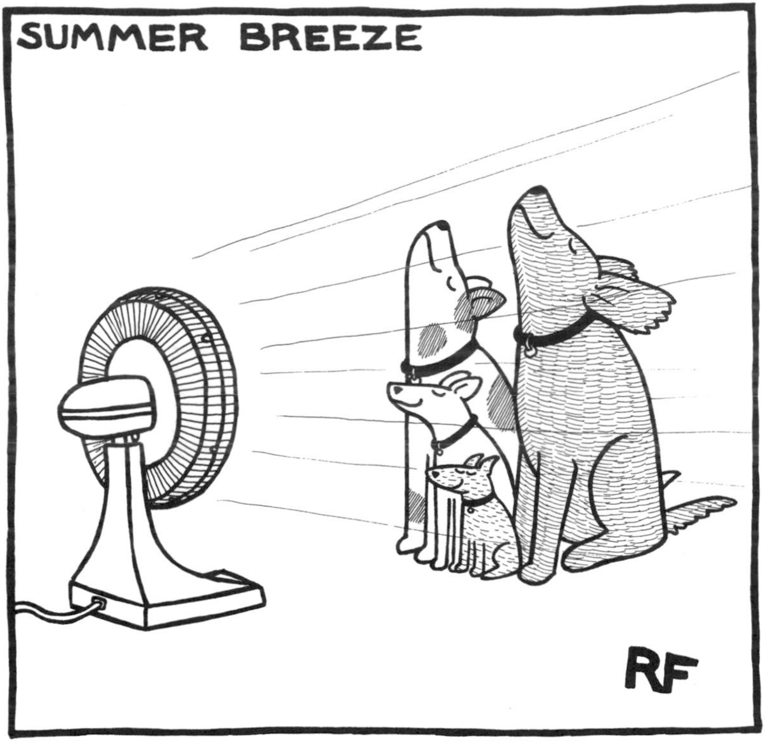
SUMMER BREEZE
RF

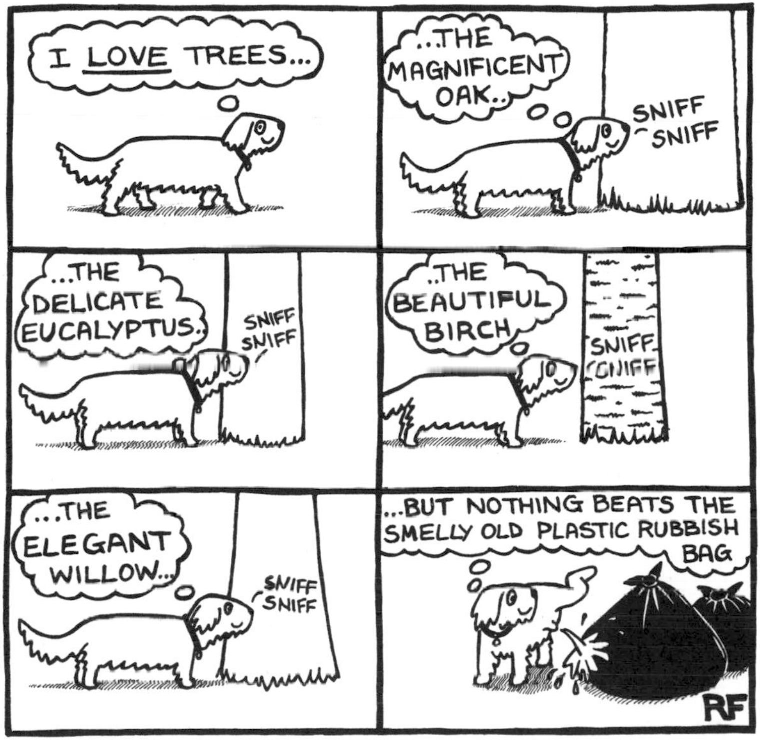
I LOVE TREES...
..THE MAGNIFICENT OAK..
SNIFF SNIFF
...THE DELICATE EUCALYPTUS..
SNIFF SNIFF
..THE BEAUTIFUL BIRCH
SNIFF SNIFF
...THE ELEGANT WILLOW..
SNIFF SNIFF
...BUT NOTHING BEATS THE SMELLY OLD PLASTIC RUBBISH BAG
RF

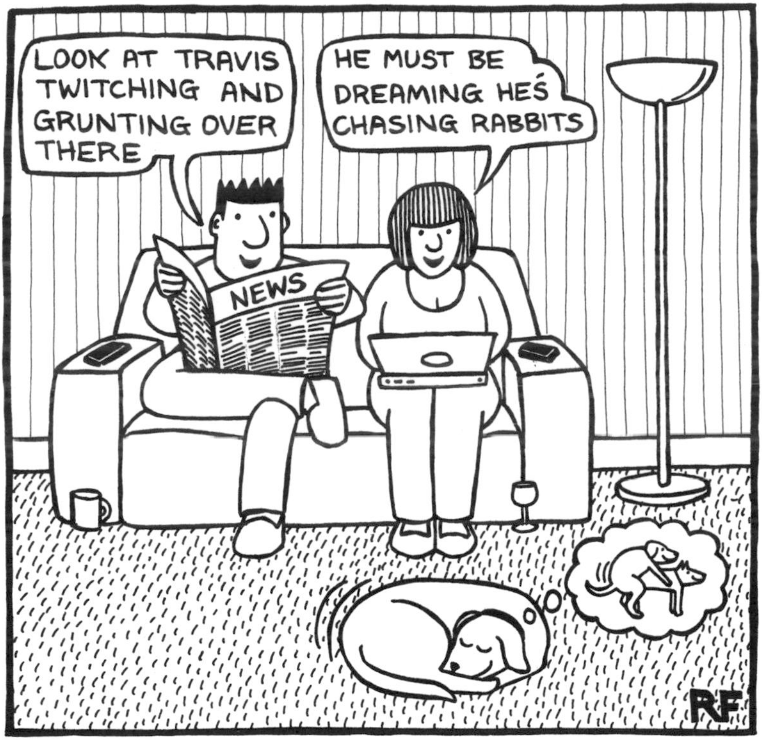
LOOK AT TRAVIS TWITCHING AND GRUNTING OVER THERE
HE MUST BE DREAMING HE'S CHASING RABBITS
NEWS
RF

LIVING WITH LEONBERGERS...

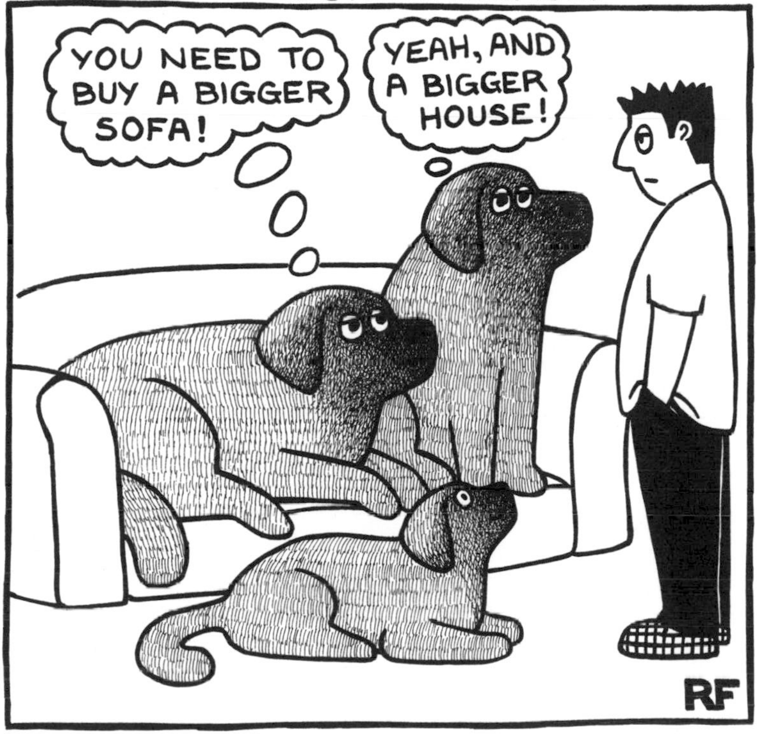
YOU NEED TO BUY A BIGGER SOFA!
YEAH, AND A BIGGER HOUSE!
RF

AT THE CANINE CAFE...

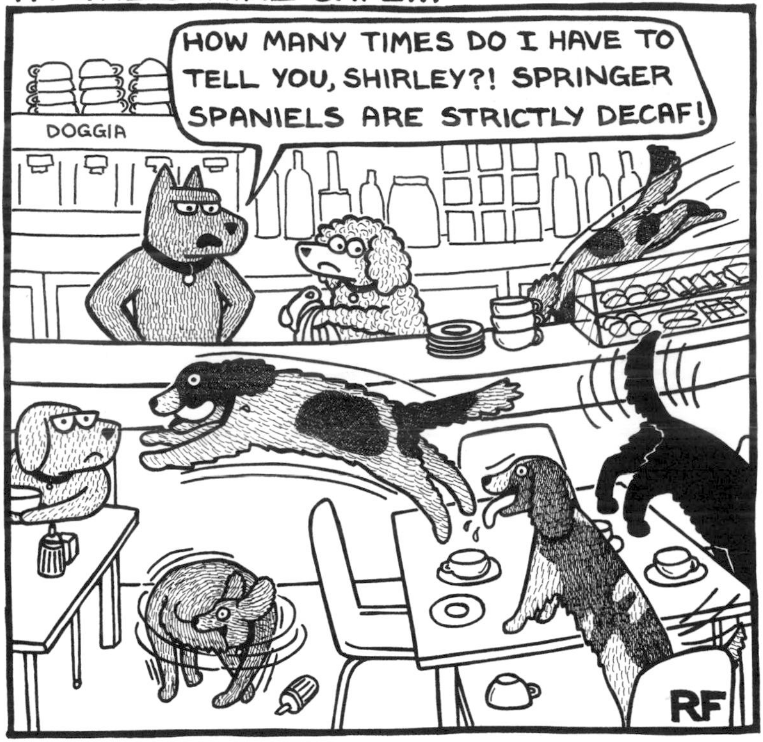
HOW MANY TIMES DO I HAVE TO TELL YOU, SHIRLEY?! SPRINGER SPANIELS ARE STRICTLY DECAF!
DOGGIA
RF

THE NEW PUPPY...

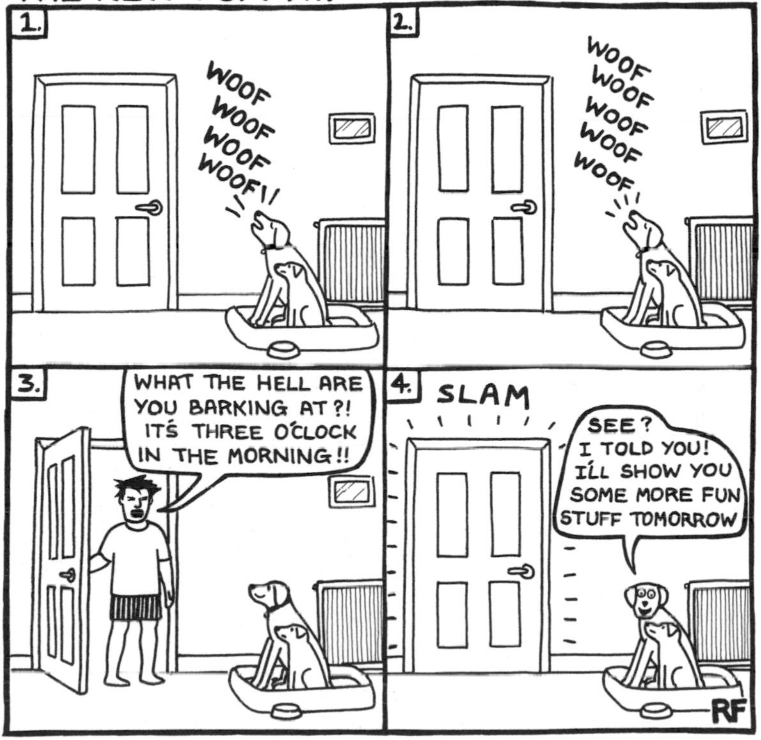
1.
WOOF WOOF WOOF WOOF!!
2.
WOOF WOOF WOOF WOOF WOOF
3.
WHAT THE HELL ARE YOU BARKING AT?! ITŚ THREE O'CLOCK IN THE MORNING!!
4.
SLAM
SEE? I TOLD YOU! IĹL SHOW YOU SOME MORE FUN STUFF TOMORROW
RF

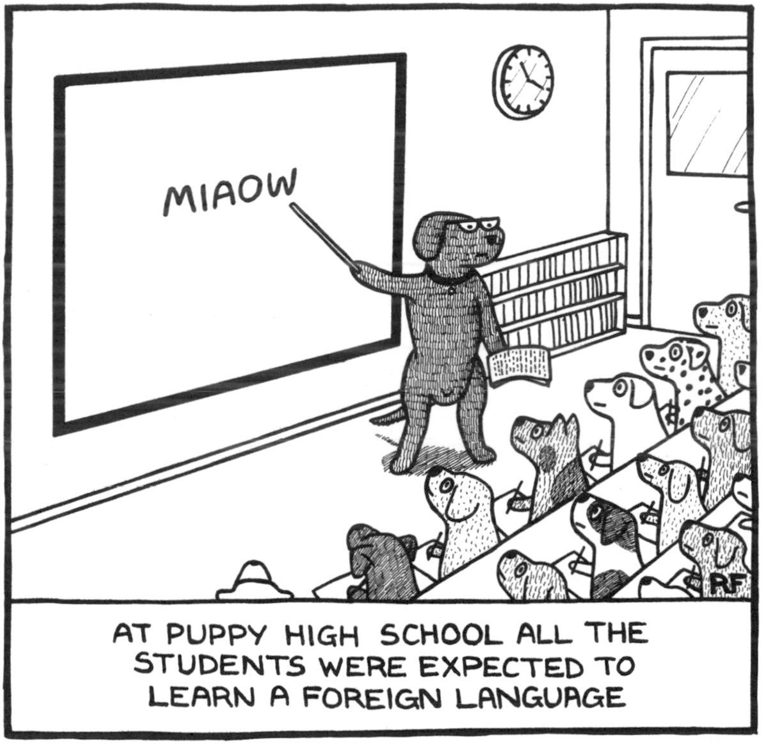
MIAOW
RF

AT PUPPY HIGH SCHOOL ALL THE STUDENTS WERE EXPECTED TO LEARN A FOREIGN LANGUAGE

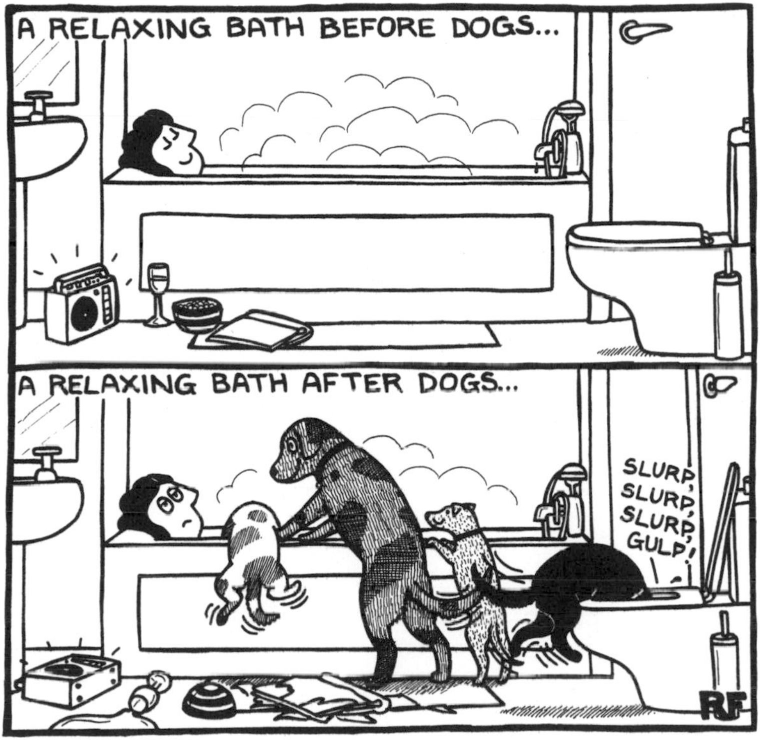
A RELAXING BATH BEFORE DOGS...
A RELAXING BATH AFTER DOGS...
SLURP, SLURP, SLURP, GULP!
RF

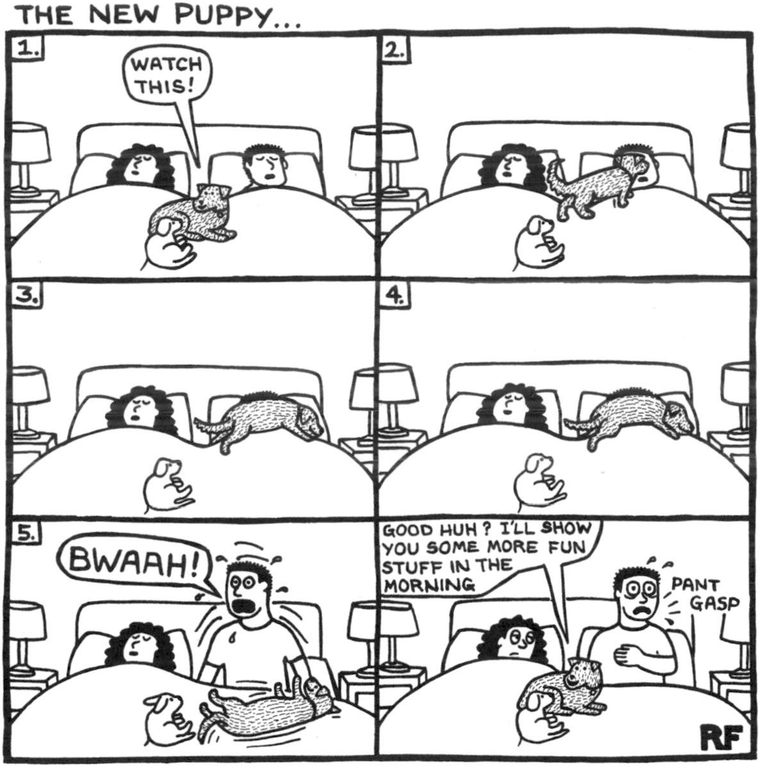
THE NEW PUPPY...
1.
WATCH THIS!
2.
3.
4.
5.
BWAAH!
GOOD HUH ? I'LL SHOW YOU SOME MORE FUN STUFF IN THE MORNING
PANT GASP
RF

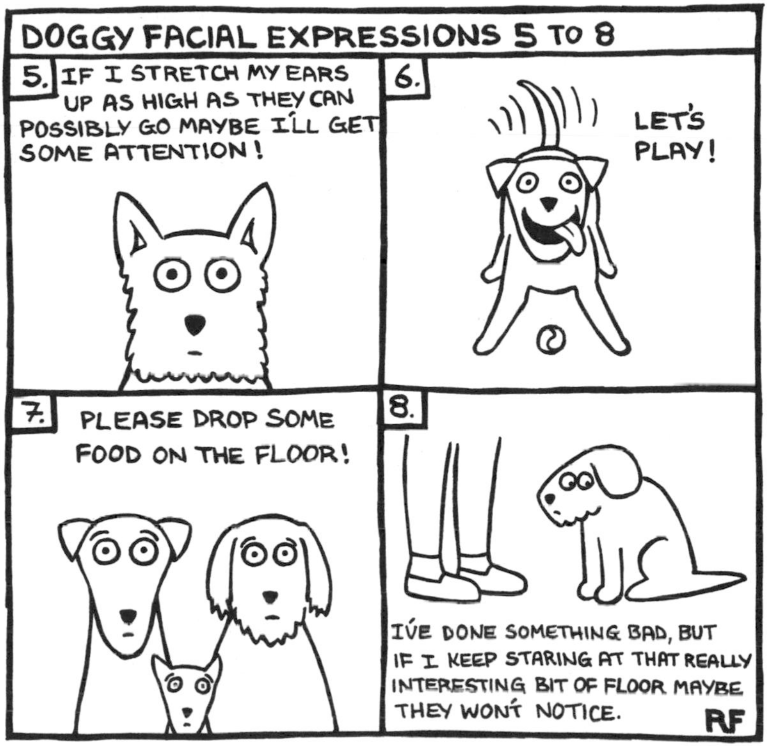
DOGGY FACIAL EXPRESSIONS 5 TO 8
5.
IF I STRETCH MY EARS UP AS HIGH AS THEY CAN POSSIBLY GO MAYBE I'LL GET SOME ATTENTION!
6.
LET'S PLAY!
7.
PLEASE DROP SOME FOOD ON THE FLOOR!
8.
I'VE DONE SOMETHING BAD, BUT IF I KEEP STARING AT THAT REALLY INTERESTING BIT OF FLOOR MAYBE THEY WON'T NOTICE.
RF

THE S.W.A.T. TEAM...

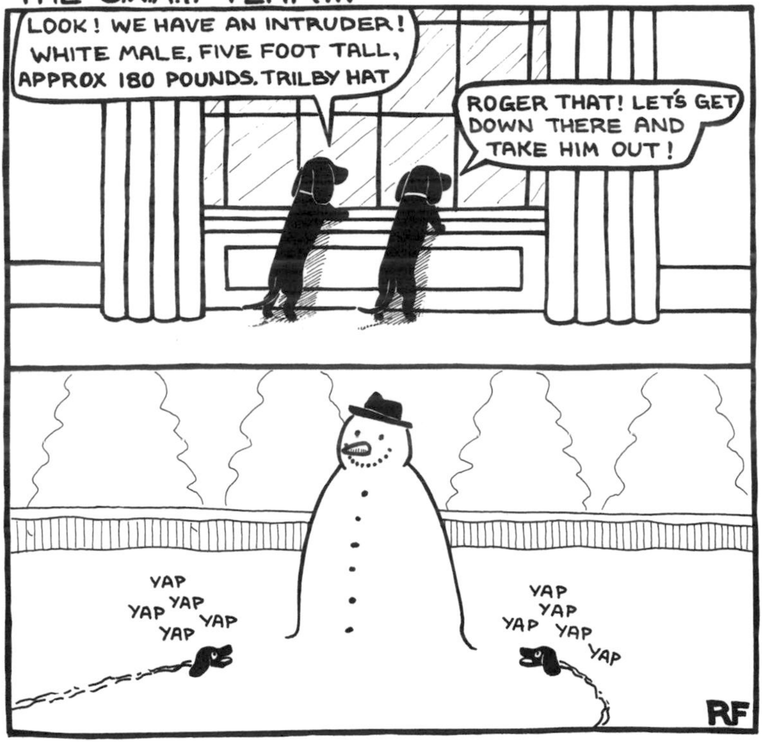
LOOK! WE HAVE AN INTRUDER! WHITE MALE, FIVE FOOT TALL, APPROX 180 POUNDS. TRILBY HAT
ROGER THAT! LET'S GET DOWN THERE AND TAKE HIM OUT!
YAP YAP YAP YAP YAP
YAP YAP YAP YAP YAP
RF

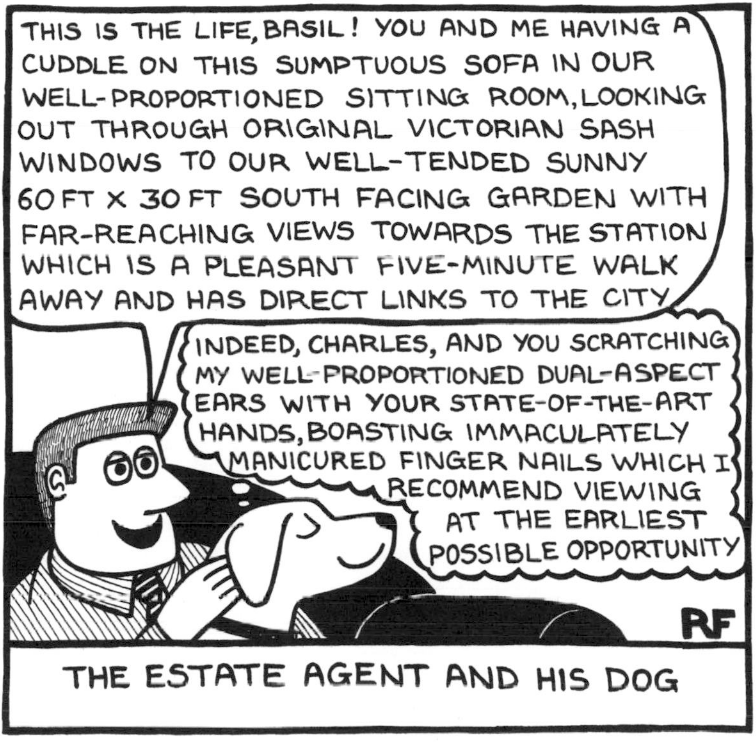
THIS IS THE LIFE, BASIL! YOU AND ME HAVING A CUDDLE ON THIS SUMPTUOUS SOFA IN OUR WELL-PROPORTIONED SITTING ROOM, LOOKING OUT THROUGH ORIGINAL VICTORIAN SASH WINDOWS TO OUR WELL-TENDED SUNNY 60 FT X 30 FT SOUTH FACING GARDEN WITH FAR-REACHING VIEWS TOWARDS THE STATION WHICH IS A PLEASANT FIVE-MINUTE WALK AWAY AND HAS DIRECT LINKS TO THE CITY
INDEED, CHARLES, AND YOU SCRATCHING MY WELL-PROPORTIONED DUAL-ASPECT EARS WITH YOUR STATE-OF-THE-ART HANDS, BOASTING IMMACULATELY MANICURED FINGER NAILS WHICH I RECOMMEND VIEWING AT THE EARLIEST POSSIBLE OPPORTUNITY
RF

THE ESTATE AGENT AND HIS DOG

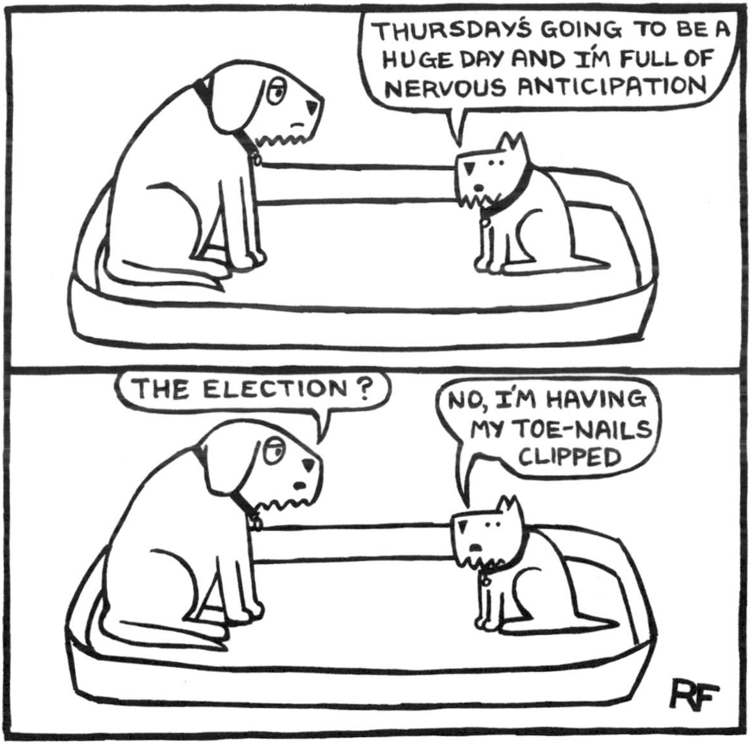
THURSDAY'S GOING TO BE A HUGE DAY AND I'M FULL OF NERVOUS ANTICIPATION
THE ELECTION?
NO, I'M HAVING MY TOE-NAILS CLIPPED
RF

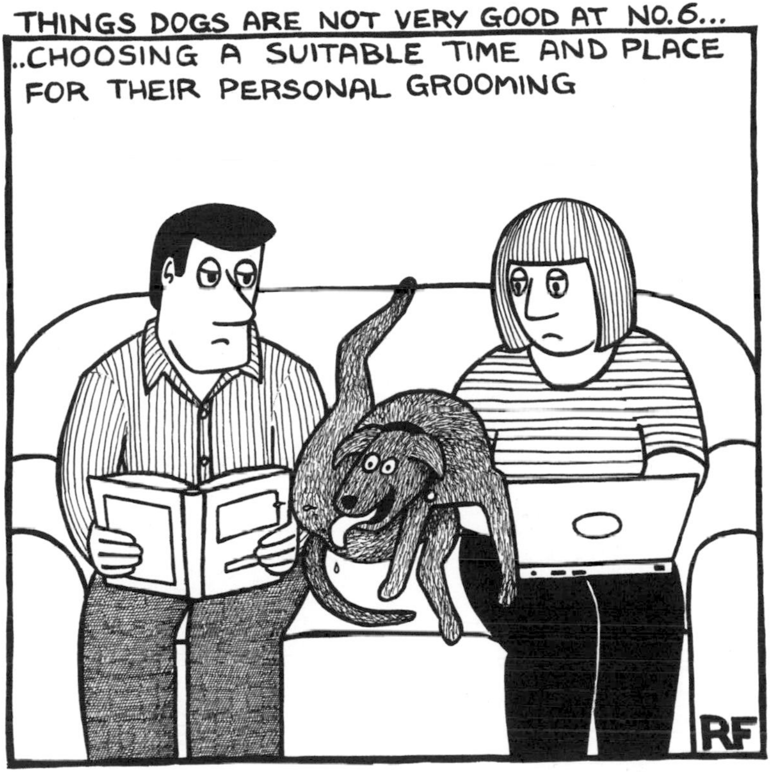
THINGS DOGS ARE NOT VERY GOOD AT NO.6...
..CHOOSING A SUITABLE TIME AND PLACE FOR THEIR PERSONAL GROOMING
RF

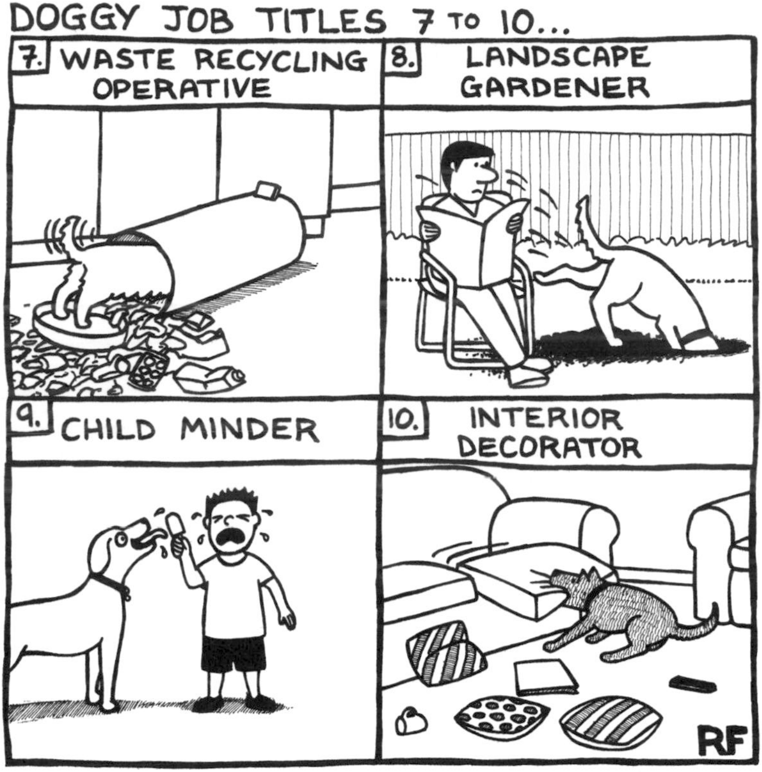
DOGGY JOB TITLES 7 TO 10...
7. WASTE RECYCLING OPERATIVE
8. LANDSCAPE GARDENER
9. CHILD MINDER
10. INTERIOR DECORATOR
RF

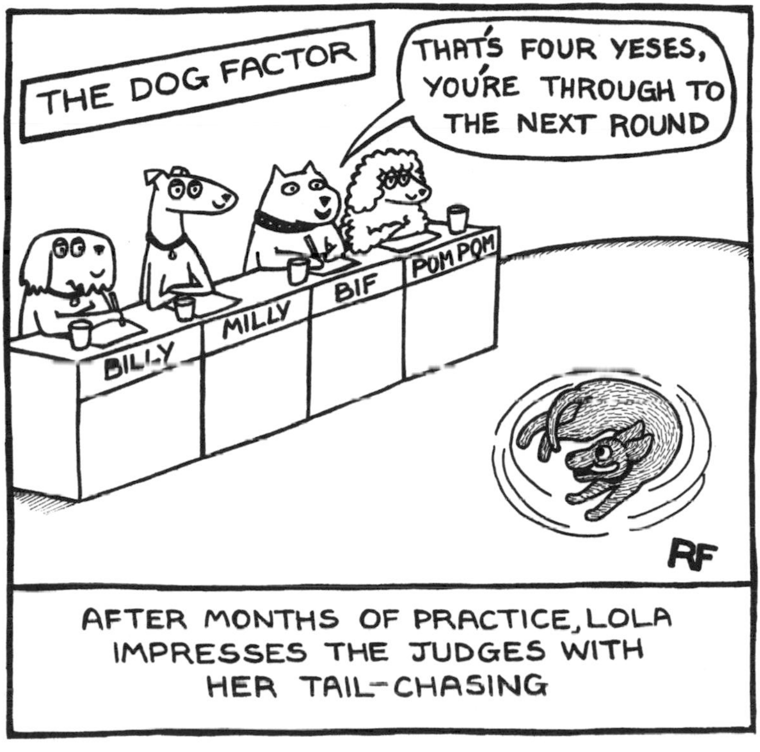
THE DOG FACTOR
THAT'S FOUR YESES, YOU'RE THROUGH TO THE NEXT ROUND
BILLY
MILLY
BIF
POM POM
RF

AFTER MONTHS OF PRACTICE, LOLA IMPRESSES THE JUDGES WITH HER TAIL-CHASING

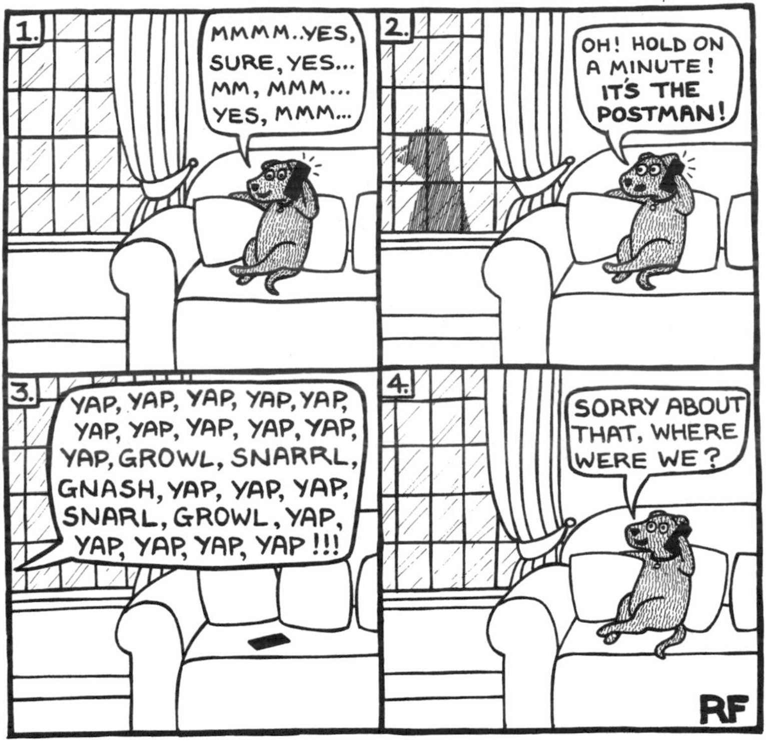
1.
MMMM..YES, SURE, YES... MM, MMM... YES, MMM...
2.
OH! HOLD ON A MINUTE! IT'S THE POSTMAN!
3.
YAP, YAP, YAP, YAP, YAP, YAP, YAP, YAP, YAP, YAP, YAP, GROWL, SNARRL, GNASH, YAP, YAP, YAP, SNARL, GROWL, YAP, YAP, YAP, YAP, YAP!!!
4.
SORRY ABOUT THAT, WHERE WERE WE?
RF

GREAT MYSTERIES OF DOG...

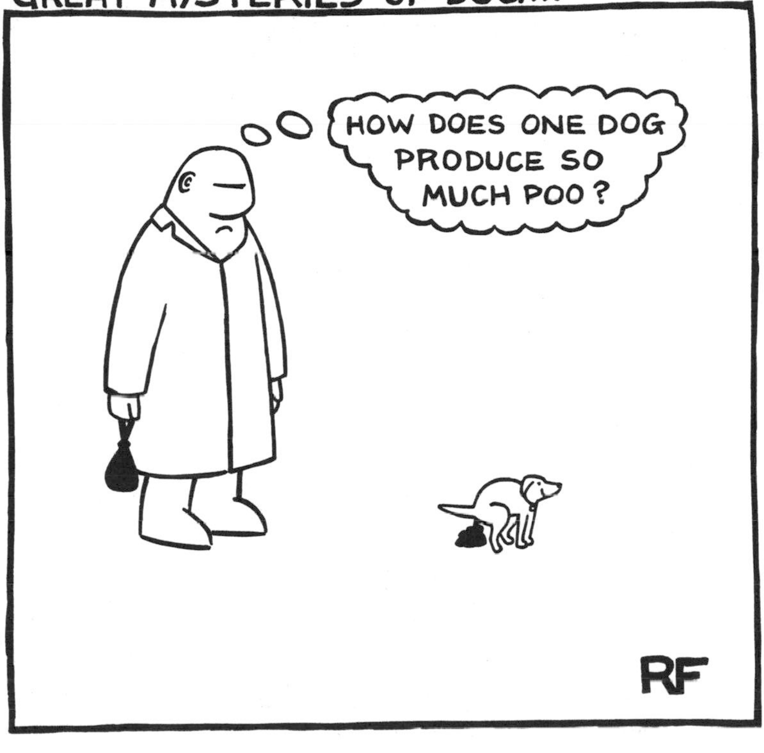
HOW DOES ONE DOG PRODUCE SO MUCH POO?
RF

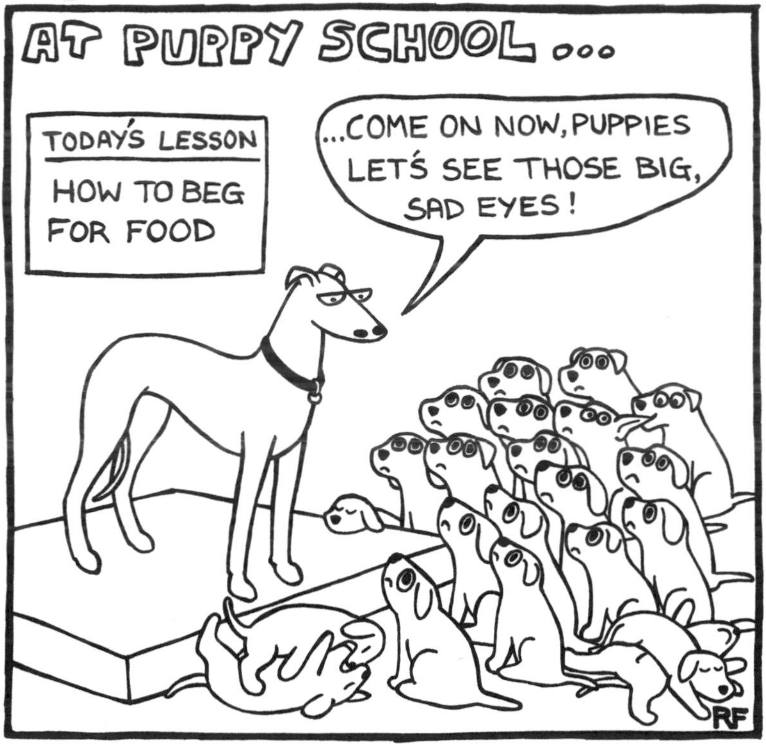
AT PUPPY SCHOOL ...
TODAY'S LESSON
HOW TO BEG FOR FOOD
...COME ON NOW, PUPPIES LET'S SEE THOSE BIG, SAD EYES!
RF

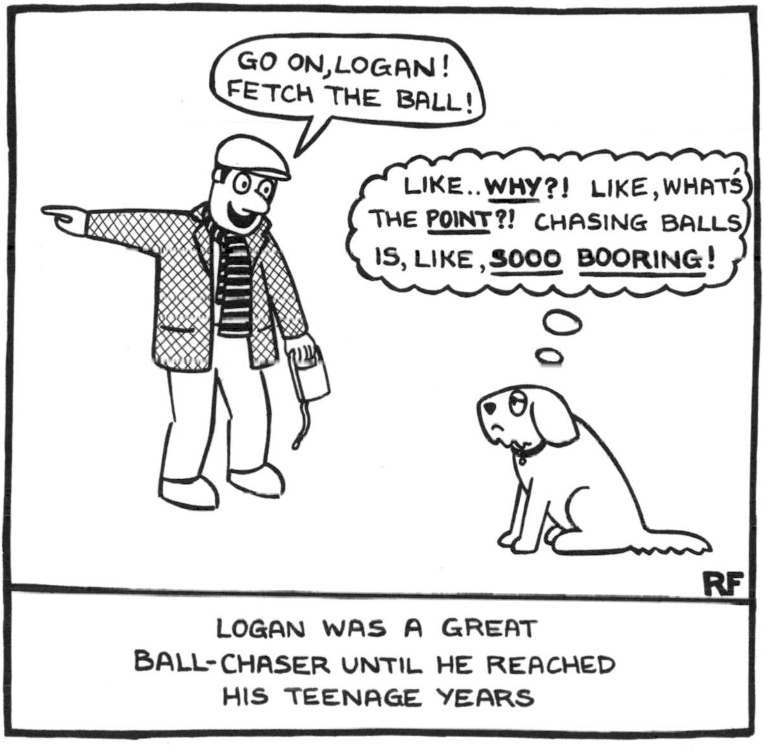
GO ON, LOGAN! FETCH THE BALL!
LIKE.. WHY?! LIKE, WHAT'S THE POINT?! CHASING BALLS IS, LIKE, SOOO BOORING!
RF

LOGAN WAS A GREAT BALL-CHASER UNTIL HE REACHED HIS TEENAGE YEARS

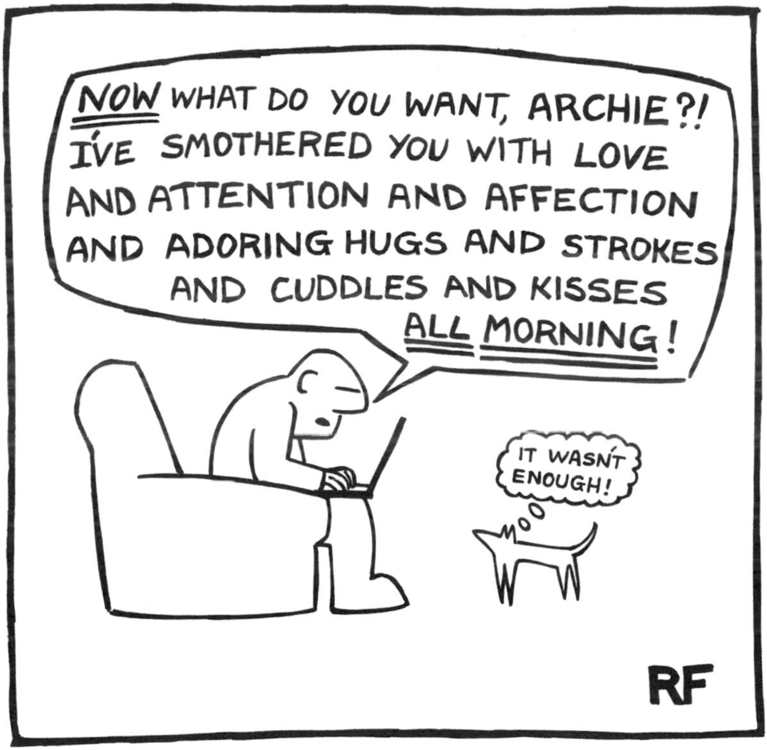
NOW WHAT DO YOU WANT, ARCHIE?! I'VE SMOTHERED YOU WITH LOVE AND ATTENTION AND AFFECTION AND ADORING HUGS AND STROKES AND CUDDLES AND KISSES ALL MORNING!
IT WASN'T ENOUGH!
RF

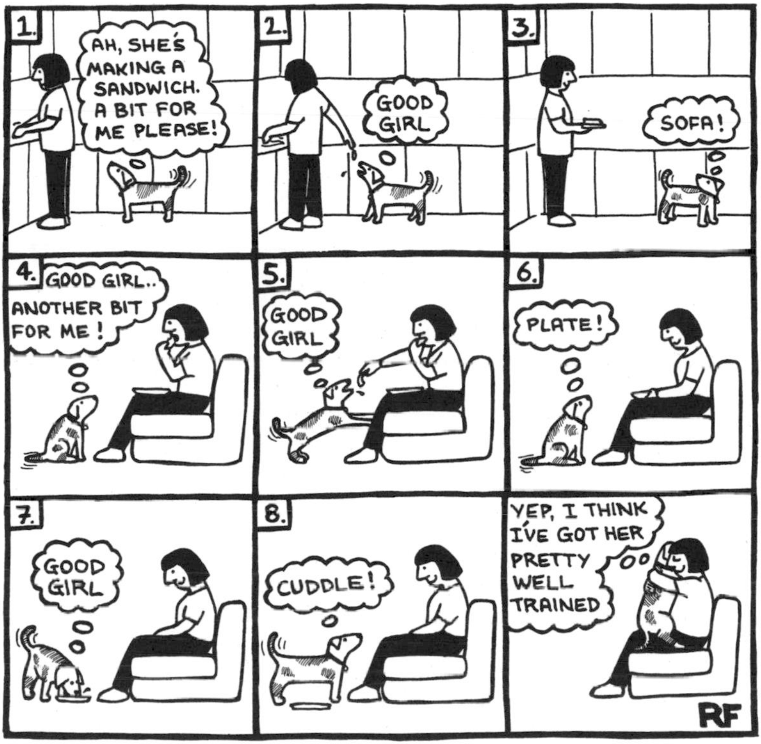
1.
AH, SHE'S MAKING A SANDWICH. A BIT FOR ME PLEASE!
2.
GOOD GIRL
3.
SOFA!
4.
GOOD GIRL.. ANOTHER BIT FOR ME!
5.
GOOD GIRL
6.
PLATE!
7.
GOOD GIRL
8.
CUDDLE!
YEP, I THINK I'VE GOT HER PRETTY WELL TRAINED
RF

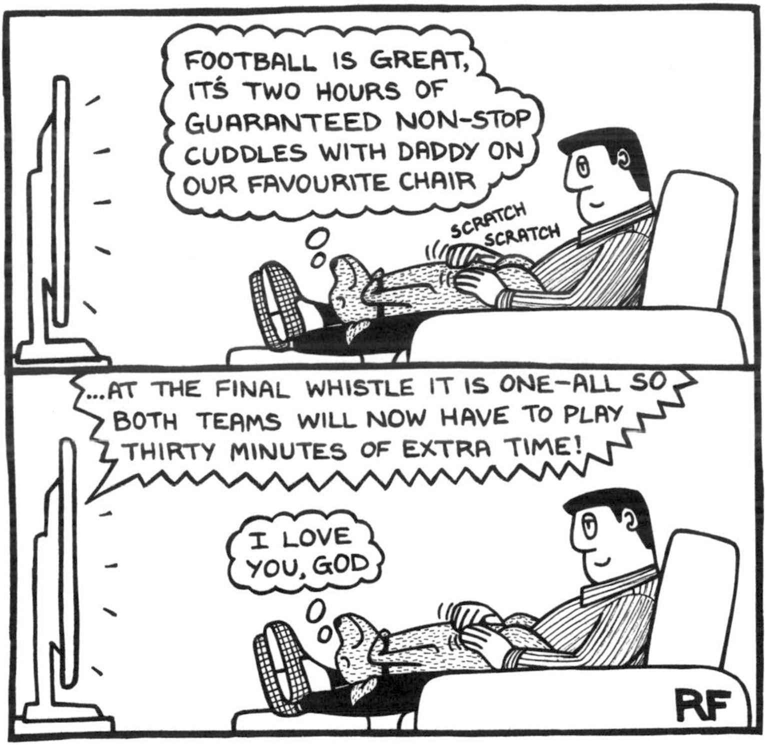
FOOTBALL IS GREAT, IT'S TWO HOURS OF GUARANTEED NON-STOP CUDDLES WITH DADDY ON OUR FAVOURITE CHAIR
SCRATCH SCRATCH
...AT THE FINAL WHISTLE IT IS ONE-ALL SO BOTH TEAMS WILL NOW HAVE TO PLAY THIRTY MINUTES OF EXTRA TIME!
I LOVE YOU, GOD
RF

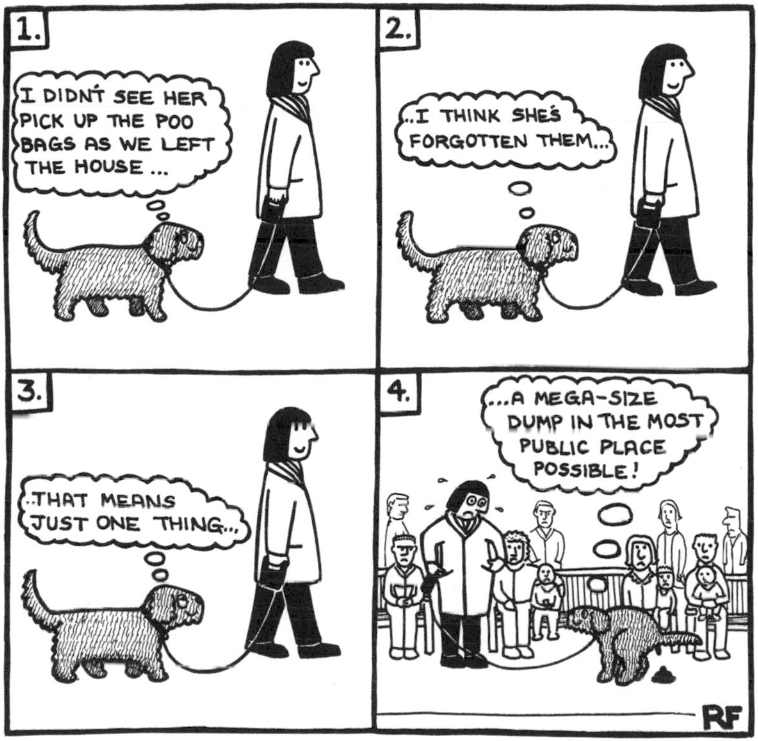
1.
I DIDN'T SEE HER PICK UP THE POO BAGS AS WE LEFT THE HOUSE ...
2.
..I THINK SHE'S FORGOTTEN THEM...
3.
..THAT MEANS JUST ONE THING...
4.
...A MEGA-SIZE DUMP IN THE MOST PUBLIC PLACE POSSIBLE!
RF

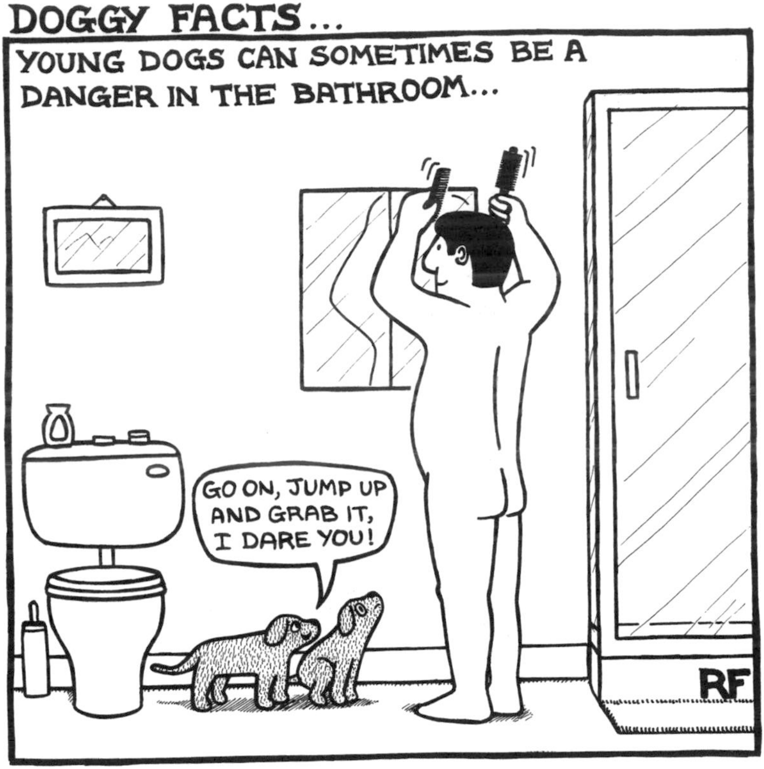
DOGGY FACTS...
YOUNG DOGS CAN SOMETIMES BE A DANGER IN THE BATHROOM...
GO ON, JUMP UP AND GRAB IT, I DARE YOU!
RF

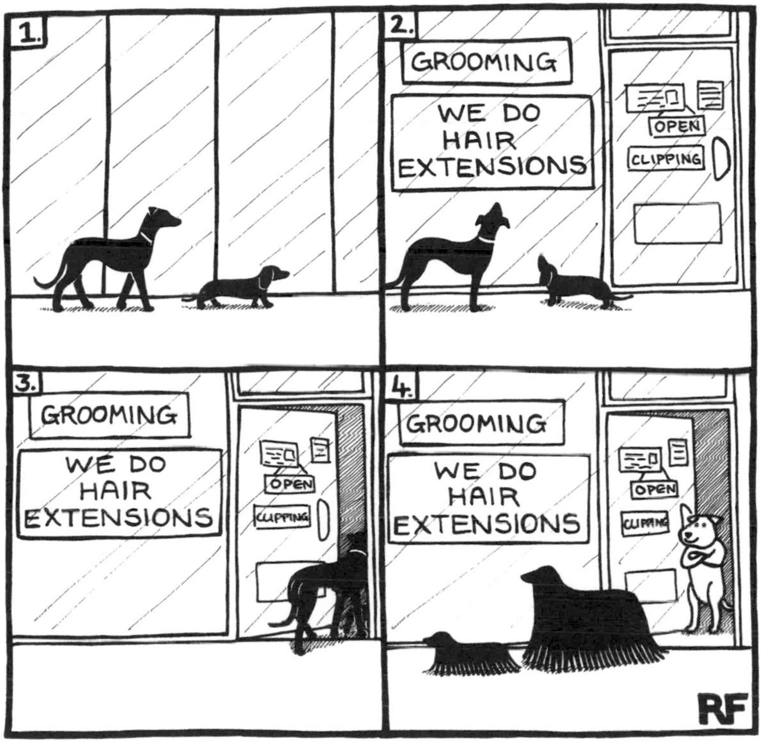
1.
2.
GROOMING
WE DO HAIR EXTENSIONS
OPEN
CLIPPING
3.
GROOMING
WE DO HAIR EXTENSIONS
OPEN
CLIPPING
4.
GROOMING
WE DO HAIR EXTENSIONS
OPEN
CLIPPING
RF

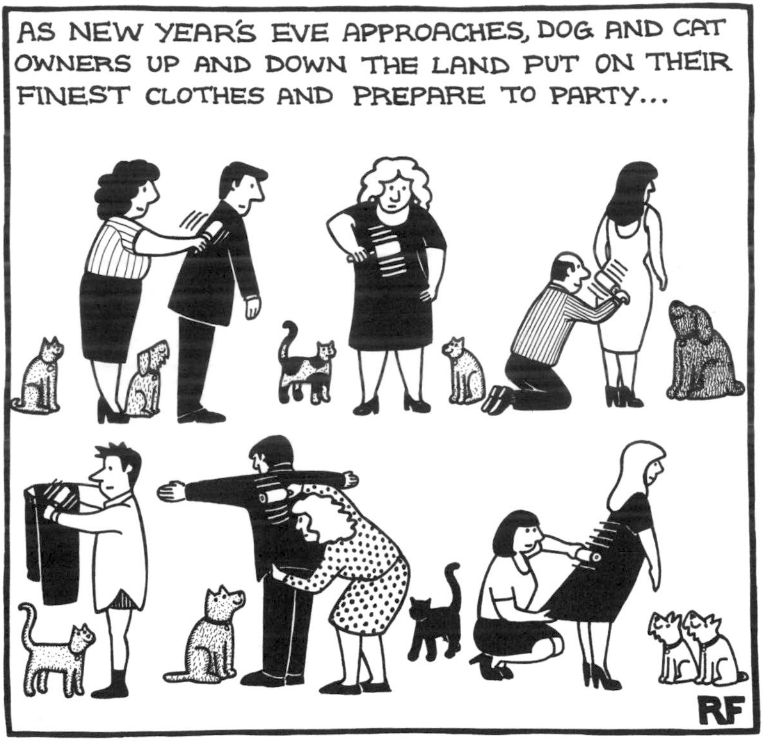
AS NEW YEAR'S EVE APPROACHES, DOG AND CAT OWNERS UP AND DOWN THE LAND PUT ON THEIR FINEST CLOTHES AND PREPARE TO PARTY...
RF

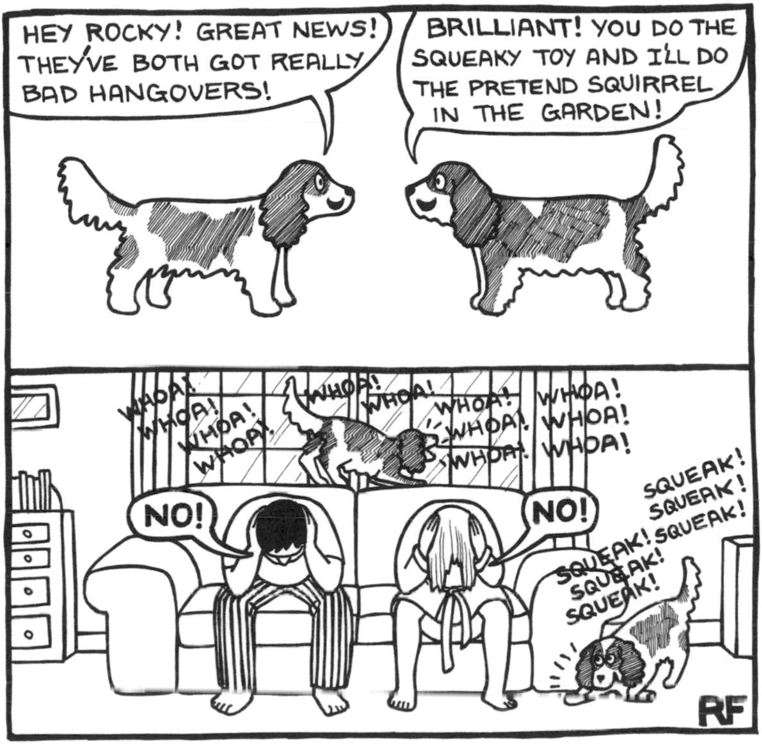
HEY ROCKY! GREAT NEWS! THEY'VE BOTH GOT REALLY BAD HANGOVERS!
BRILLIANT! YOU DO THE SQUEAKY TOY AND I'LL DO THE PRETEND SQUIRREL IN THE GARDEN!
WHOA! WHOA! WHOA! WHOA! WHOA! WHOA! WHOA! WHOA! WHOA! WHOA! WHOA! WHOA! WHOA!
NO!
NO!
SQUEAK! SQUEAK! SQUEAK! SQUEAK! SQUEAK! SQUEAK!
RF

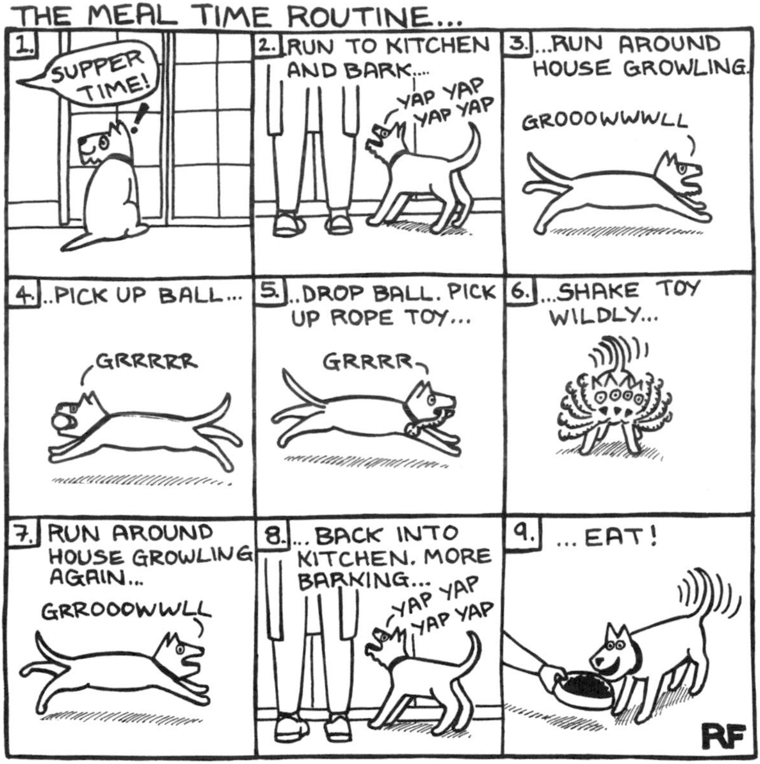
THE MEAL TIME ROUTINE...
1.
SUPPER TIME!
!
2. RUN TO KITCHEN AND BARK....
YAP YAP YAP YAP
3. ...RUN AROUND HOUSE GROWLING.
GROOOWWWLL
4. ..PICK UP BALL...
GRRRRR
5. ..DROP BALL. PICK UP ROPE TOY...
GRRRR
6. ...SHAKE TOY WILDLY...
7. RUN AROUND HOUSE GROWLING AGAIN...
GRROOOWWLL
8. ... BACK INTO KITCHEN. MORE BARKING...
YAP YAP YAP YAP
9. ... EAT!
RF

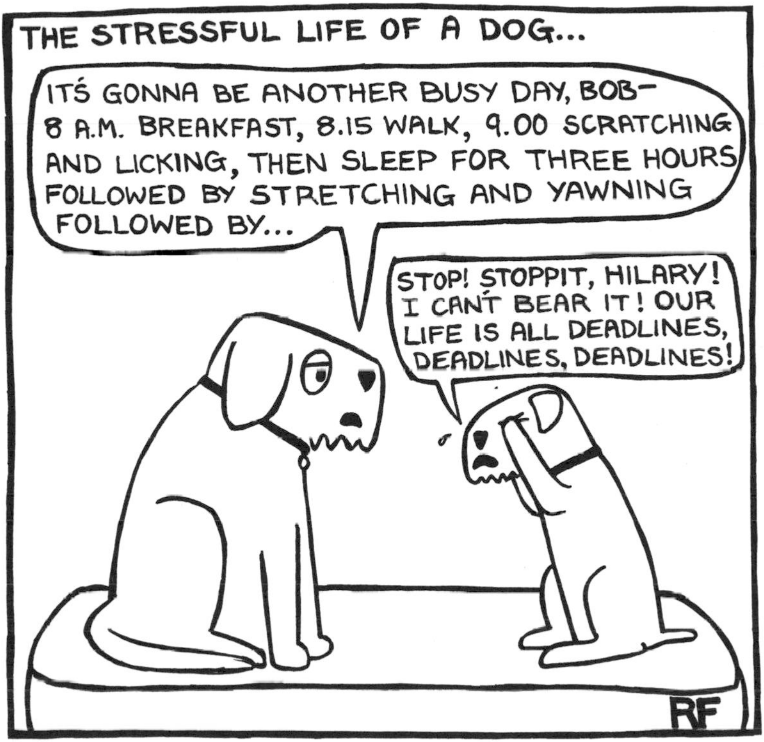
THE STRESSFUL LIFE OF A DOG...
ITS GONNA BE ANOTHER BUSY DAY, BOB– 8 A.M. BREAKFAST, 8.15 WALK, 9.00 SCRATCHING AND LICKING, THEN SLEEP FOR THREE HOURS FOLLOWED BY STRETCHING AND YAWNING FOLLOWED BY...
STOP! STOPPIT, HILARY! I CAN'T BEAR IT! OUR LIFE IS ALL DEADLINES, DEADLINES, DEADLINES!
RF

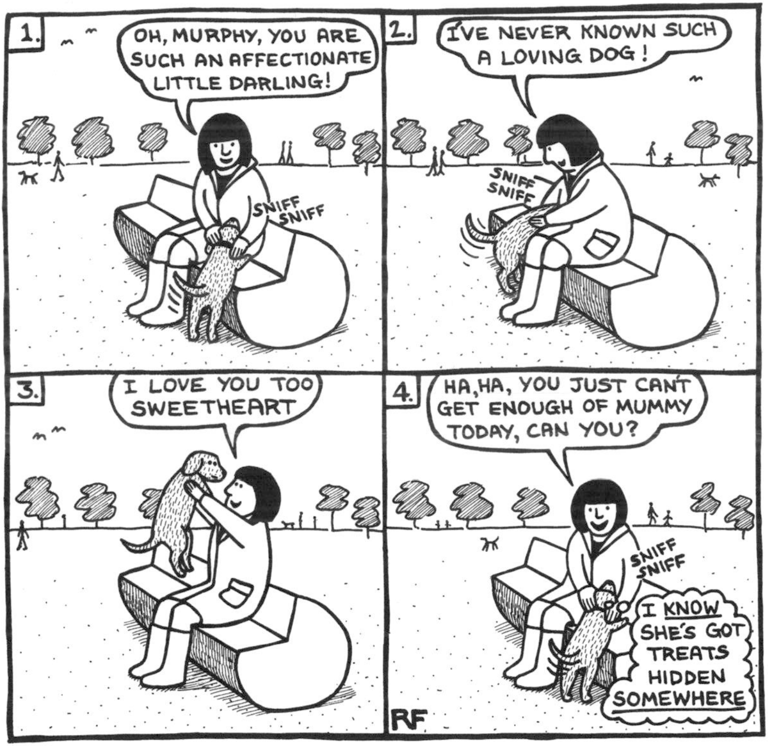
1.
OH, MURPHY, YOU ARE SUCH AN AFFECTIONATE LITTLE DARLING!
SNIFF SNIFF
2.
I'VE NEVER KNOWN SUCH A LOVING DOG!
SNIFF SNIFF
3.
I LOVE YOU TOO SWEETHEART
4.
HA, HA, YOU JUST CAN'T GET ENOUGH OF MUMMY TODAY, CAN YOU?
SNIFF SNIFF
I KNOW SHE'S GOT TREATS HIDDEN SOMEWHERE
RF

THE MEALTIME STARE...

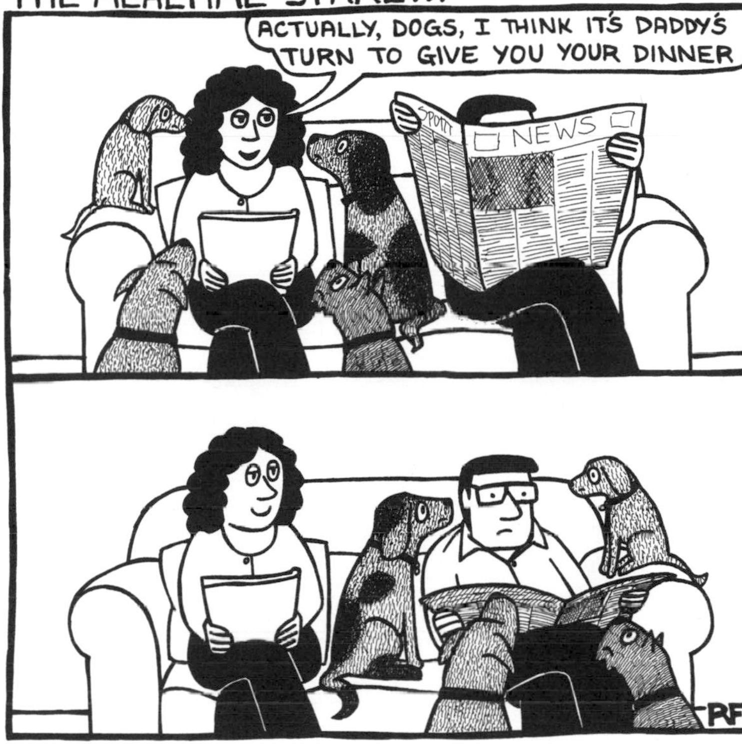
ACTUALLY, DOGS, I THINK IT'S DADDY'S TURN TO GIVE YOU YOUR DINNER
NEWS
RF

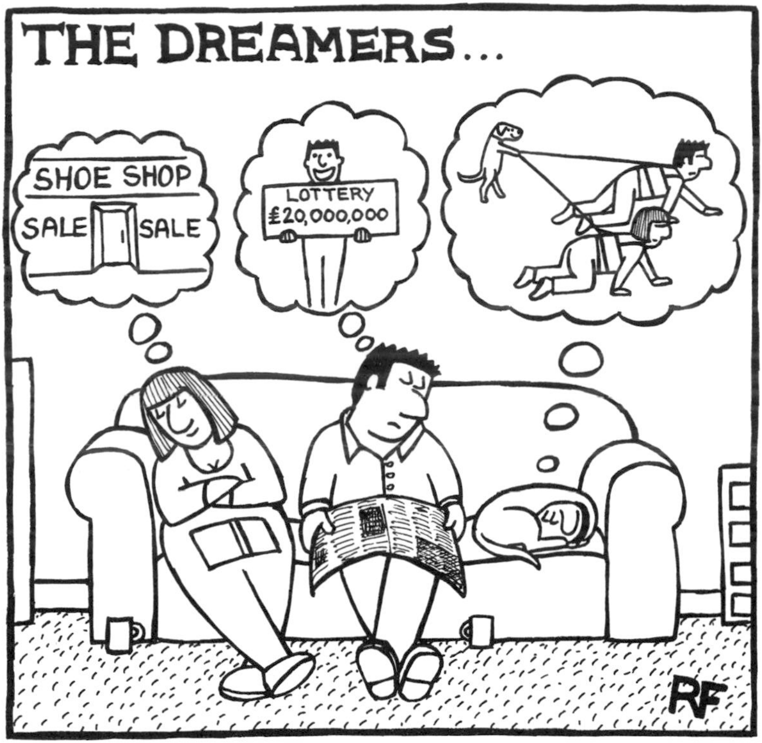
THE DREAMERS...
SHOE SHOP
SALE
SALE
LOTTERY
£20,000,000
RF

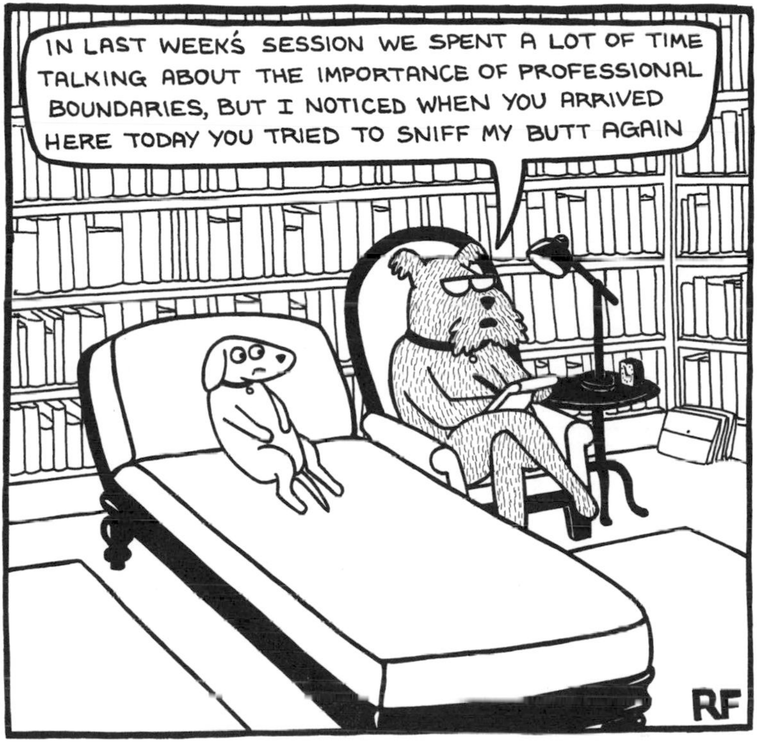
IN LAST WEEK'S SESSION WE SPENT A LOT OF TIME TALKING ABOUT THE IMPORTANCE OF PROFESSIONAL BOUNDARIES, BUT I NOTICED WHEN YOU ARRIVED HERE TODAY YOU TRIED TO SNIFF MY BUTT AGAIN
RF

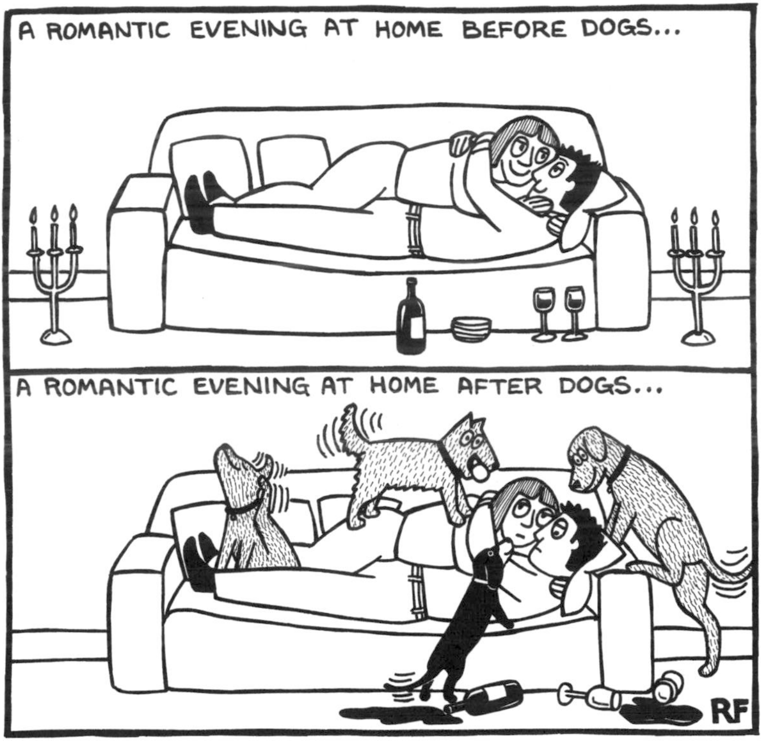
A ROMANTIC EVENING AT HOME BEFORE DOGS...
A ROMANTIC EVENING AT HOME AFTER DOGS...
RF

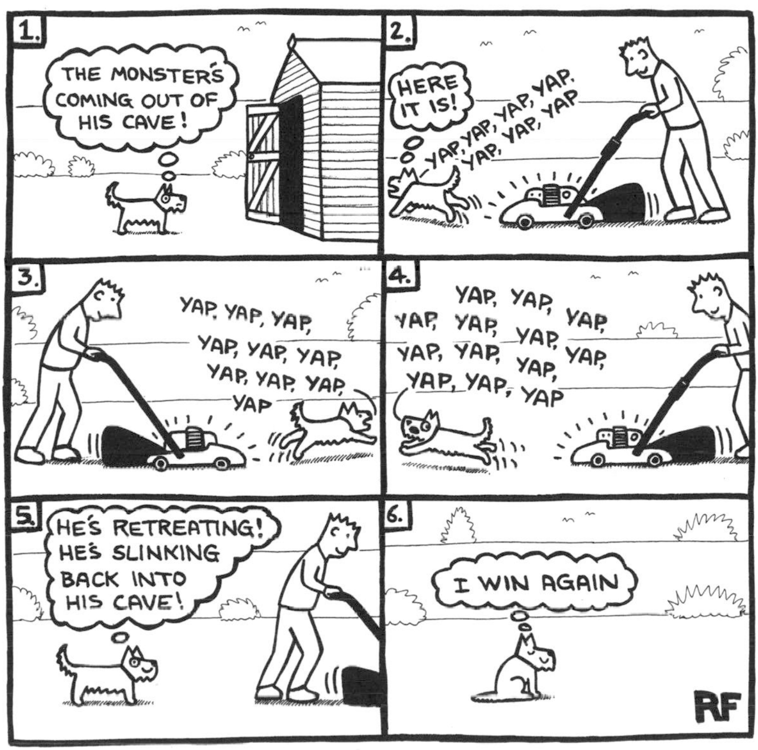
1.
THE MONSTER'S COMING OUT OF HIS CAVE!
2.
HERE IT IS!
YAP, YAP, YAP, YAP, YAP, YAP, YAP, YAP
3.
YAP, YAP, YAP,
YAP, YAP, YAP,
YAP, YAP, YAP,
YAP
4.
YAP, YAP, YAP,
YAP, YAP, YAP, YAP,
YAP, YAP, YAP, YAP,
YAP, YAP, YAP
5.
HE'S RETREATING! HE'S SLINKING BACK INTO HIS CAVE!
6.
I WIN AGAIN
RF

AT PUPPY SCHOOL...

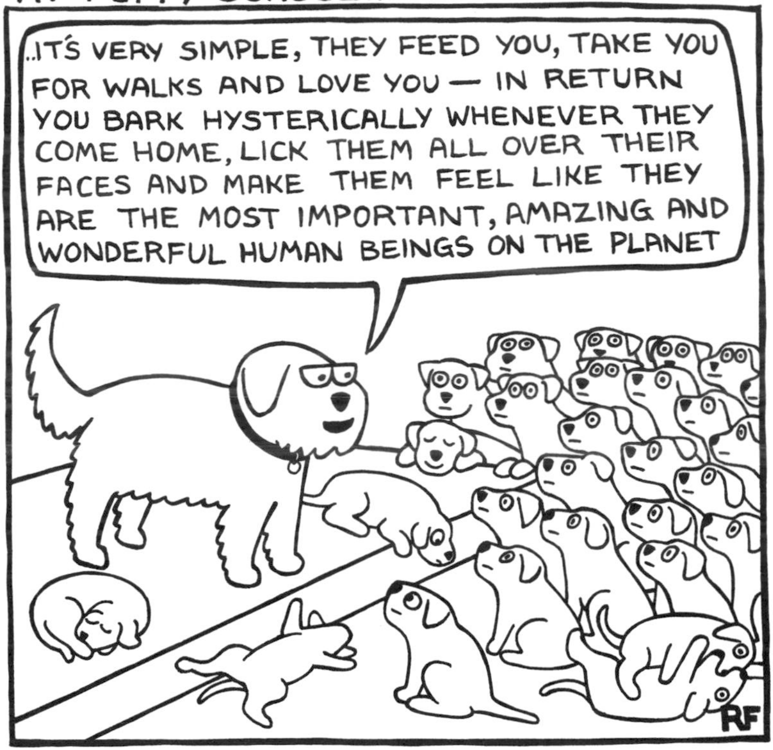
..IT'S VERY SIMPLE, THEY FEED YOU, TAKE YOU FOR WALKS AND LOVE YOU — IN RETURN YOU BARK HYSTERICALLY WHENEVER THEY COME HOME, LICK THEM ALL OVER THEIR FACES AND MAKE THEM FEEL LIKE THEY ARE THE MOST IMPORTANT, AMAZING AND WONDERFUL HUMAN BEINGS ON THE PLANET
RF

THE MULTI-PURPOSE HUMAN...
1. CHAUFFEUR
2. PERSONAL TRAINER
3. POO CARRIER
4. HAIRDRESSER
5. EAR SCRATCHER
6. HEATED BED
7. CHEF
8. WAITER
9. NAPKIN
WIPE
WIPE
RF

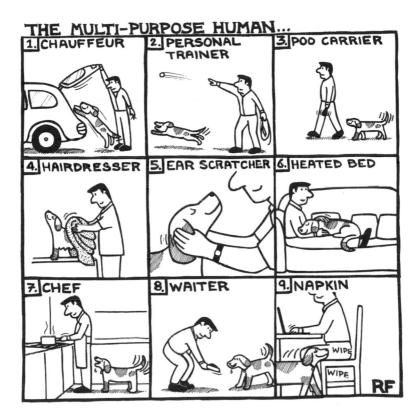

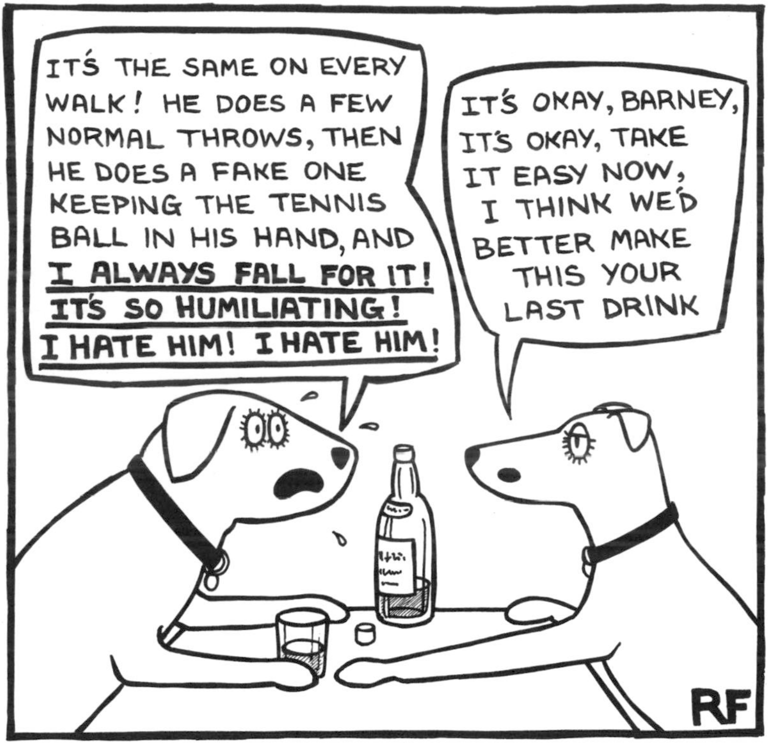
IT'S THE SAME ON EVERY WALK! HE DOES A FEW NORMAL THROWS, THEN HE DOES A FAKE ONE KEEPING THE TENNIS BALL IN HIS HAND, AND I ALWAYS FALL FOR IT! IT'S SO HUMILIATING! I HATE HIM! I HATE HIM!
IT'S OKAY, BARNEY, IT'S OKAY, TAKE IT EASY NOW, I THINK WE'D BETTER MAKE THIS YOUR LAST DRINK
RF

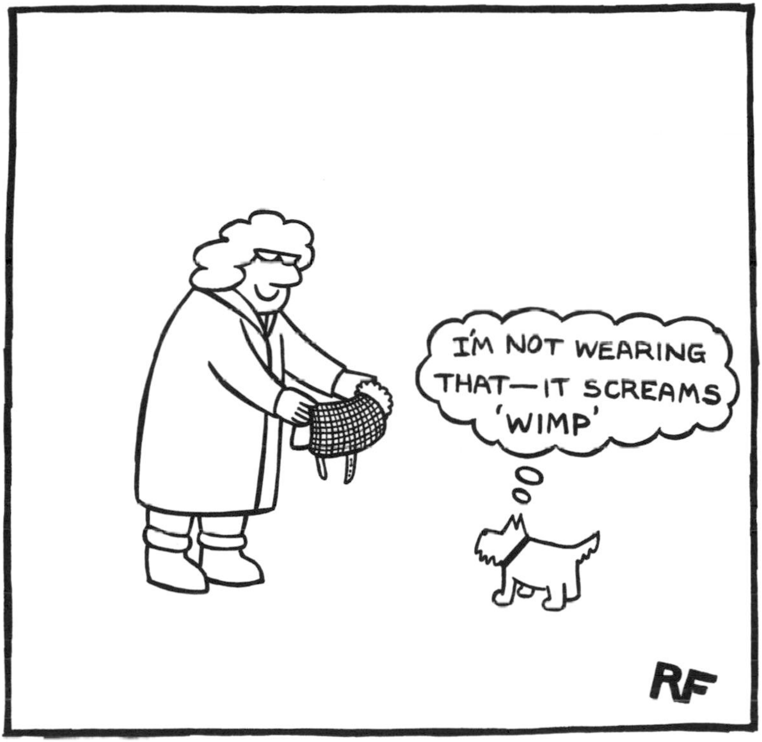
I'M NOT WEARING THAT—IT SCREAMS 'WIMP'
RF

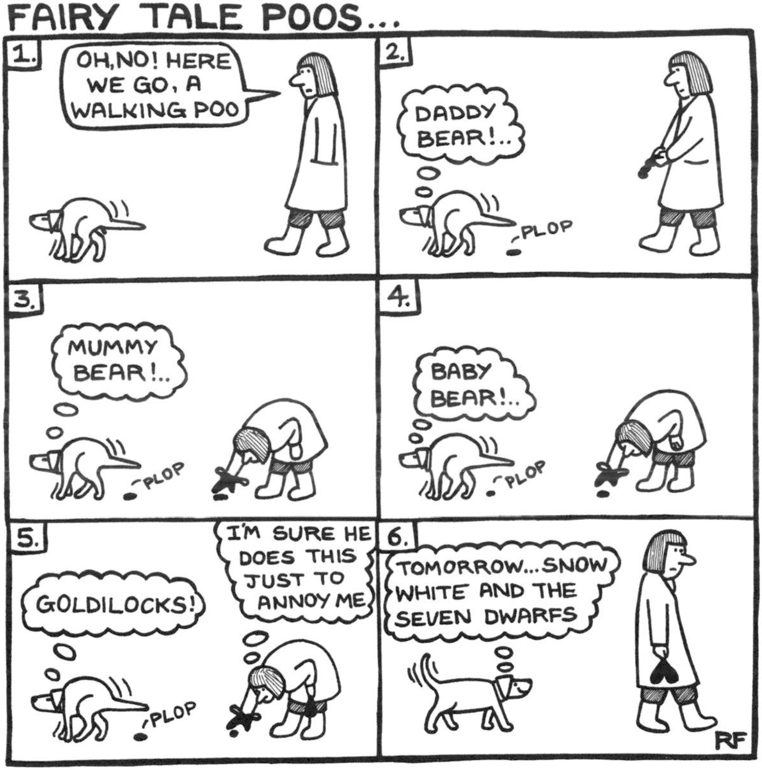
FAIRY TALE POOS...
1.
OH, NO! HERE WE GO, A WALKING POO
2.
DADDY BEAR!..
PLOP
3.
MUMMY BEAR!..
PLOP
4.
BABY BEAR!..
PLOP
5.
GOLDILOCKS!
PLOP
I'M SURE HE DOES THIS JUST TO ANNOY ME
6.
TOMORROW... SNOW WHITE AND THE SEVEN DWARFS
RF

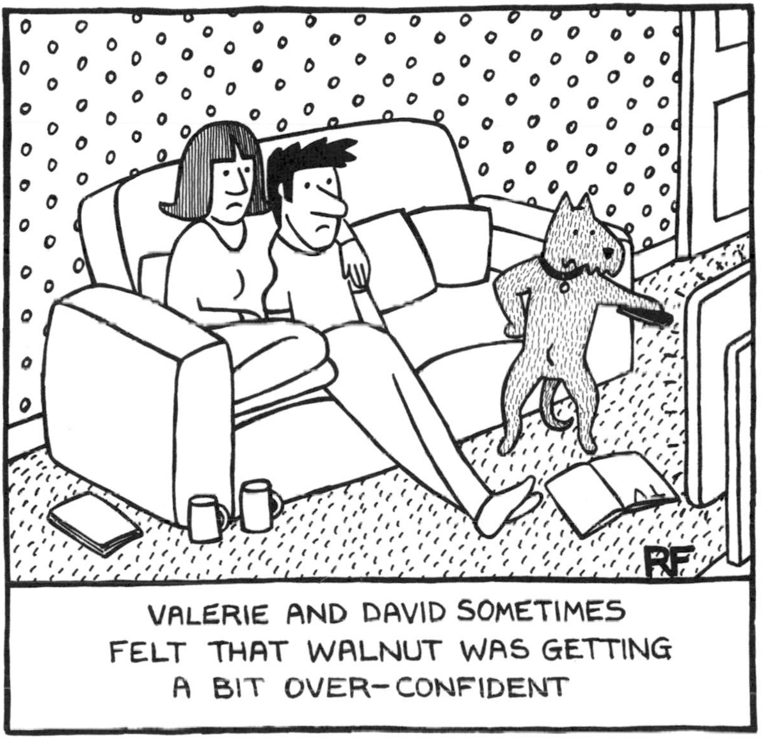
RF

VALERIE AND DAVID SOMETIMES
FELT THAT WALNUT WAS GETTING
A BIT OVER-CONFIDENT

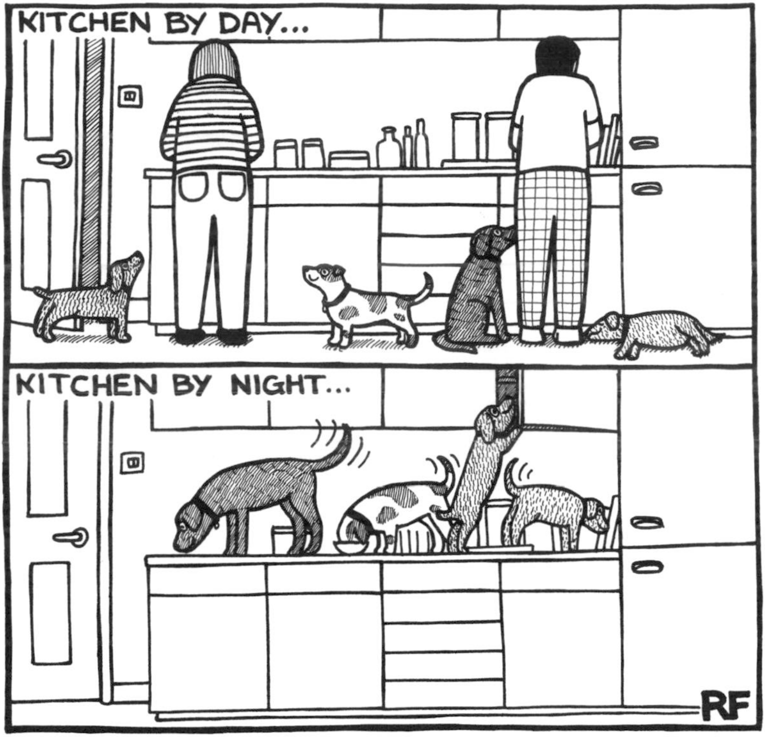
KITCHEN BY DAY...
KITCHEN BY NIGHT...
RF

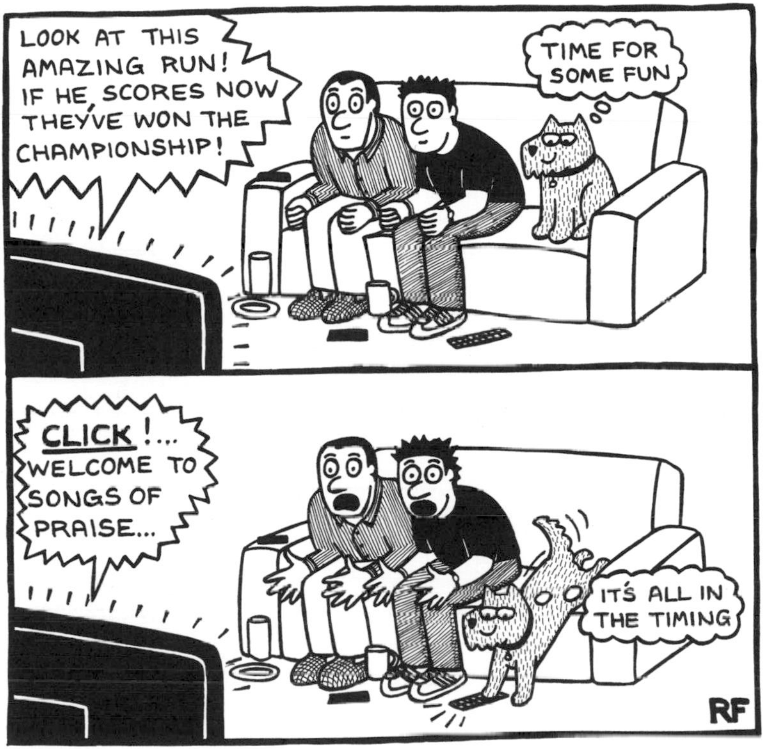
LOOK AT THIS AMAZING RUN! IF HE SCORES NOW THEY'VE WON THE CHAMPIONSHIP!
TIME FOR SOME FUN
CLICK!... WELCOME TO SONGS OF PRAISE...
IT'S ALL IN THE TIMING
RF

THE DOGFATHER...

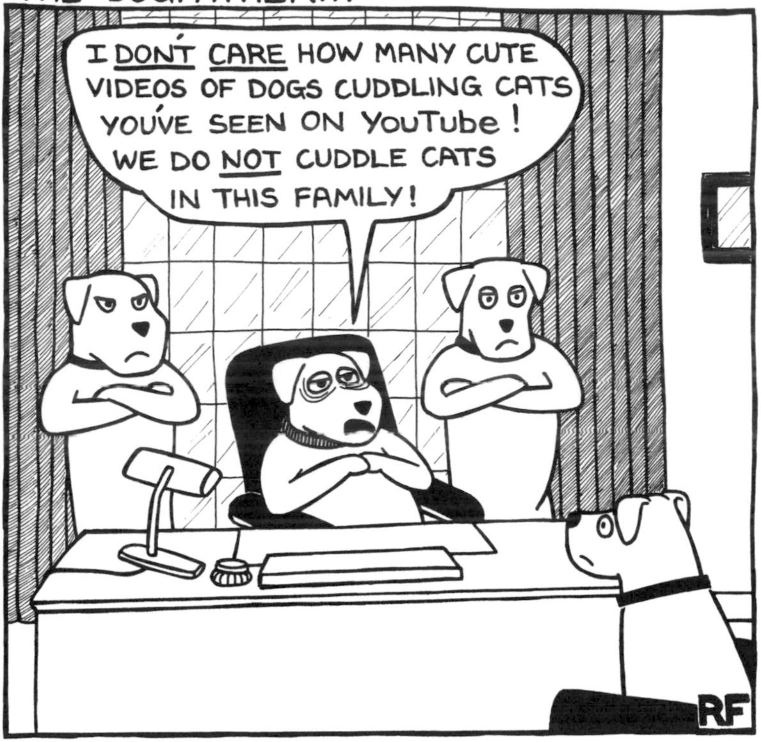
I DON'T CARE HOW MANY CUTE VIDEOS OF DOGS CUDDLING CATS YOU'VE SEEN ON YouTube! WE DO NOT CUDDLE CATS IN THIS FAMILY!
RF

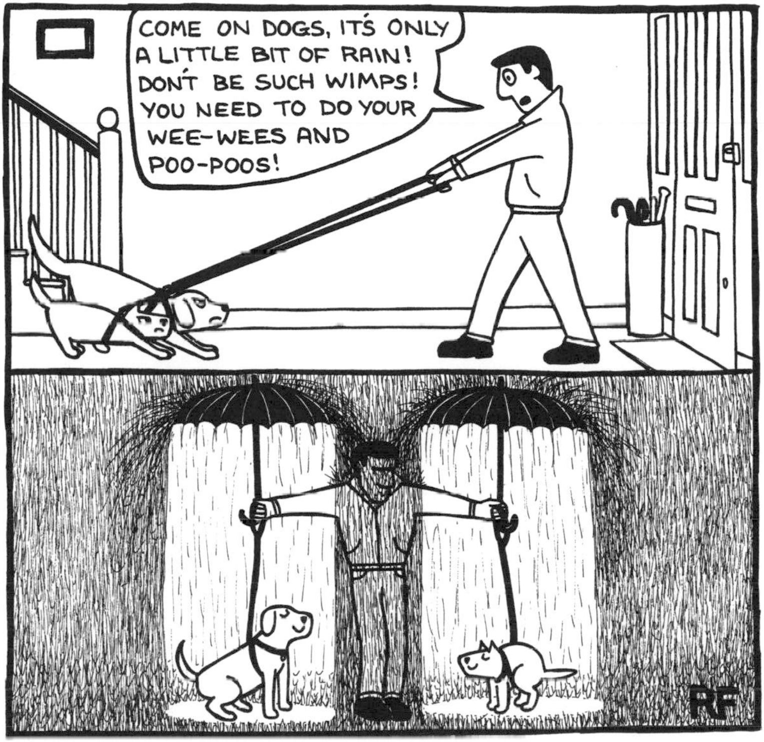
COME ON DOGS, IT'S ONLY A LITTLE BIT OF RAIN! DON'T BE SUCH WIMPS! YOU NEED TO DO YOUR WEE-WEES AND POO-POOS!
RF

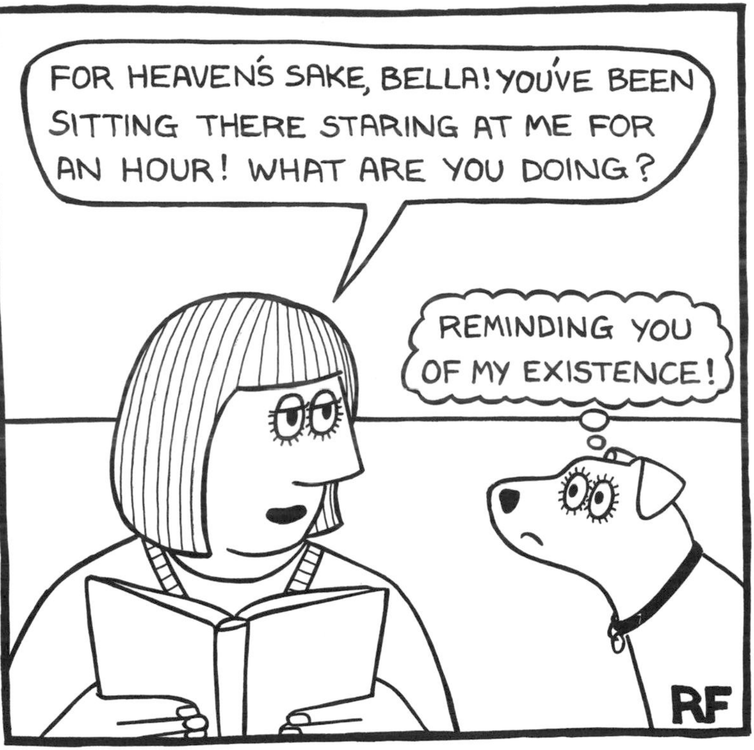
FOR HEAVEN'S SAKE, BELLA! YOU'VE BEEN SITTING THERE STARING AT ME FOR AN HOUR! WHAT ARE YOU DOING?
REMINDING YOU OF MY EXISTENCE!
RF

THE DOG PSYCHOTHERAPIST...

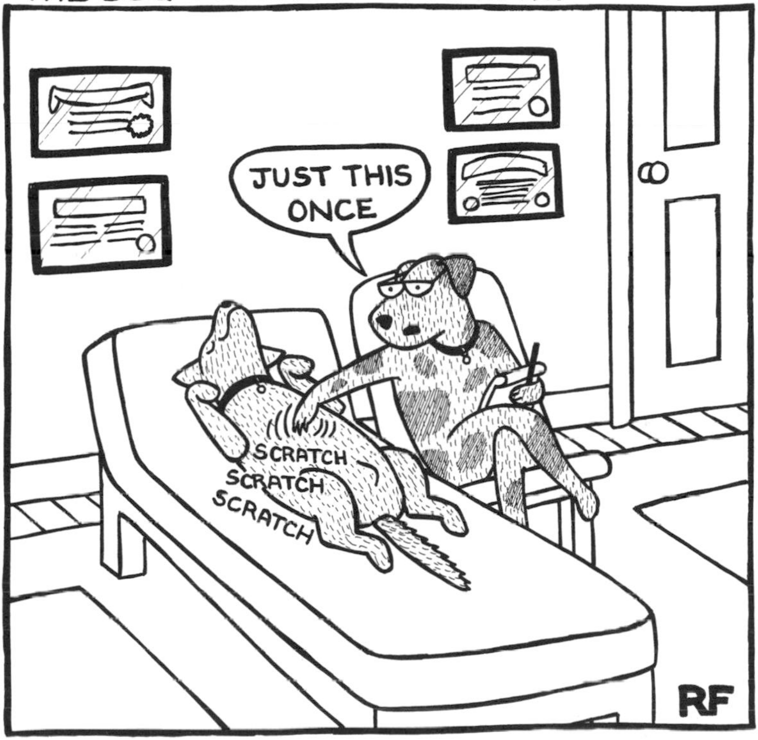
JUST THIS ONCE
SCRATCH
SCRATCH
SCRATCH
RF

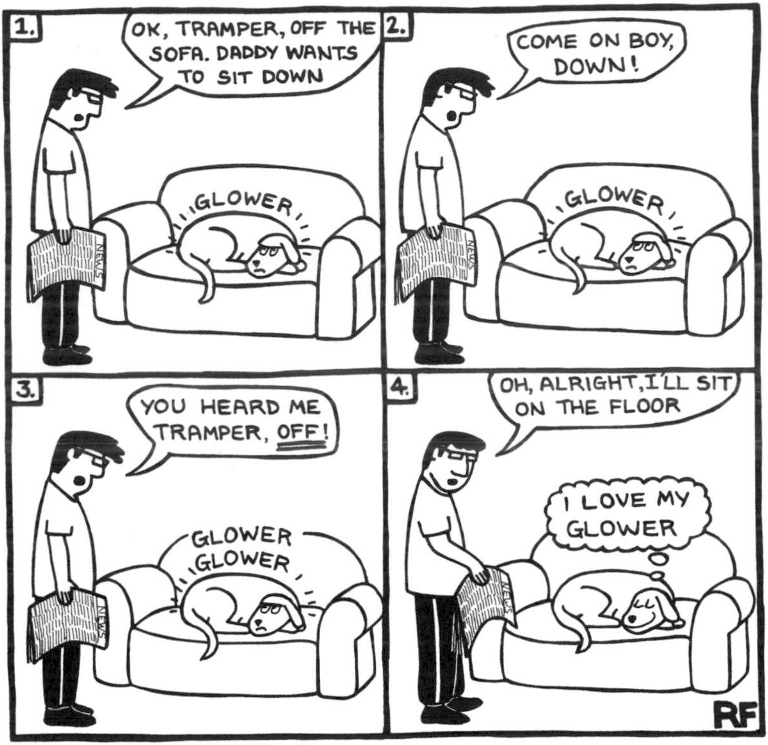
1.
OK, TRAMPER, OFF THE SOFA. DADDY WANTS TO SIT DOWN
GLOWER
NEWS
2.
COME ON BOY, DOWN!
GLOWER
NEWS
3.
YOU HEARD ME TRAMPER, OFF!
GLOWER
GLOWER
GLOWER
NEWS
4.
OH, ALRIGHT, I'LL SIT ON THE FLOOR
I LOVE MY GLOWER
NEWS
RF

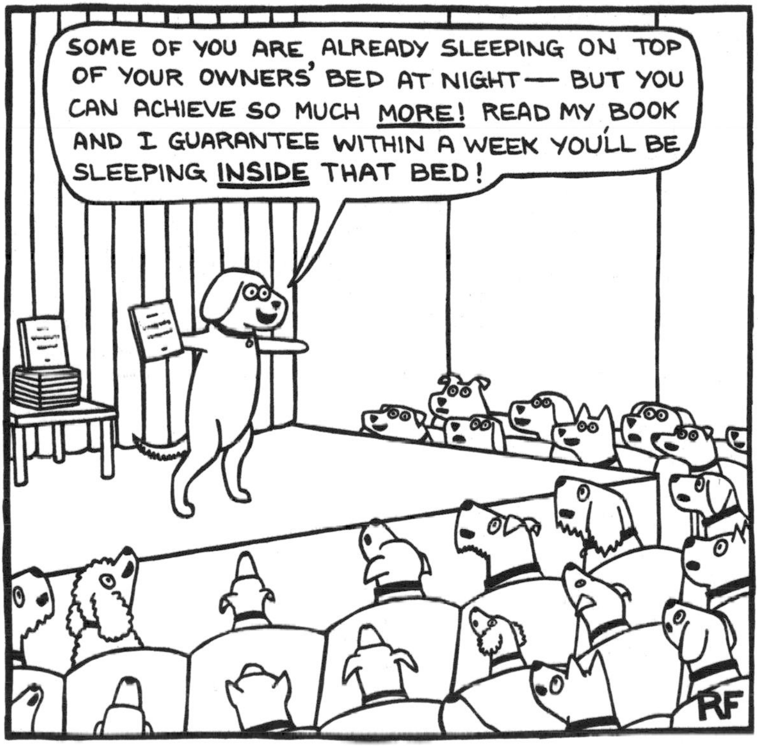
SOME OF YOU ARE ALREADY SLEEPING ON TOP OF YOUR OWNERS' BED AT NIGHT — BUT YOU CAN ACHIEVE SO MUCH MORE! READ MY BOOK AND I GUARANTEE WITHIN A WEEK YOU'LL BE SLEEPING INSIDE THAT BED!
RF

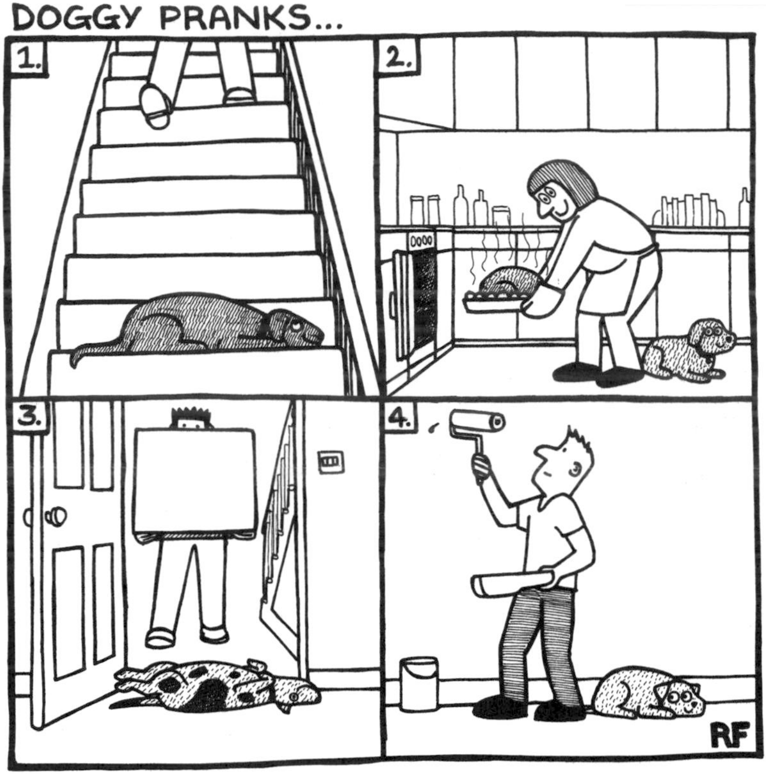
DOGGY PRANKS...
1.
2.
3.
4.
RF

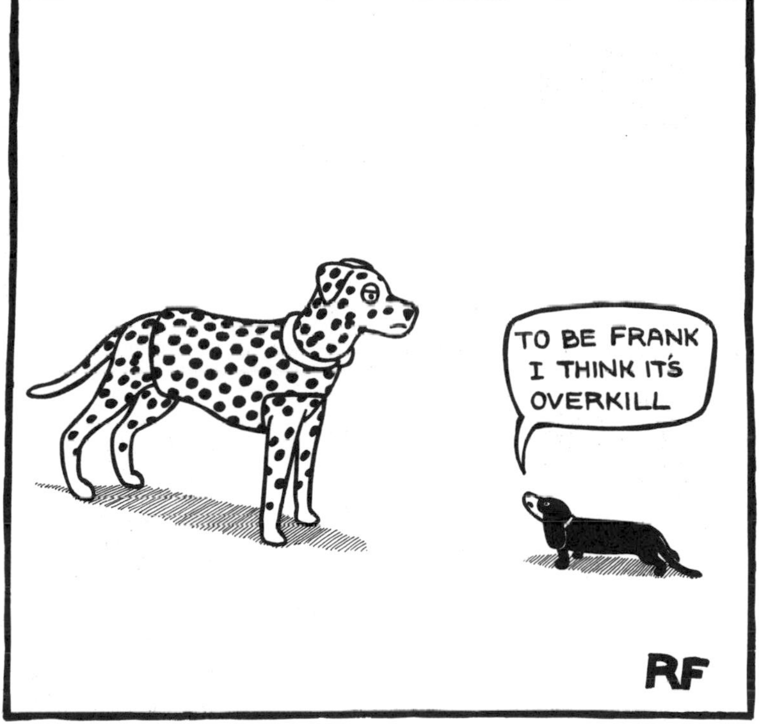
TO BE FRANK
I THINK IT'S
OVERKILL
RF

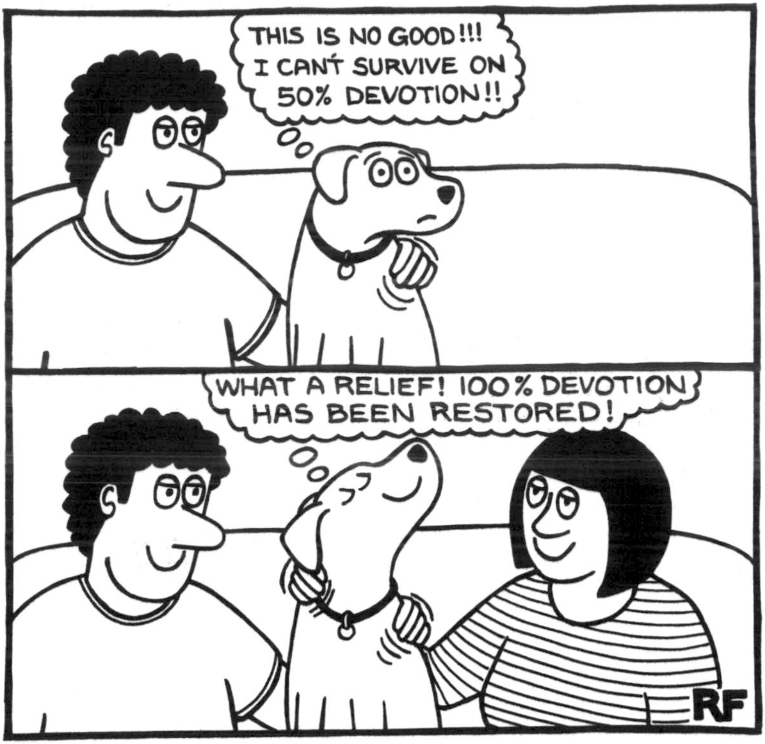
THIS IS NO GOOD!!!
I CAN'T SURVIVE ON
50% DEVOTION!!
WHAT A RELIEF! 100% DEVOTION
HAS BEEN RESTORED!
RF

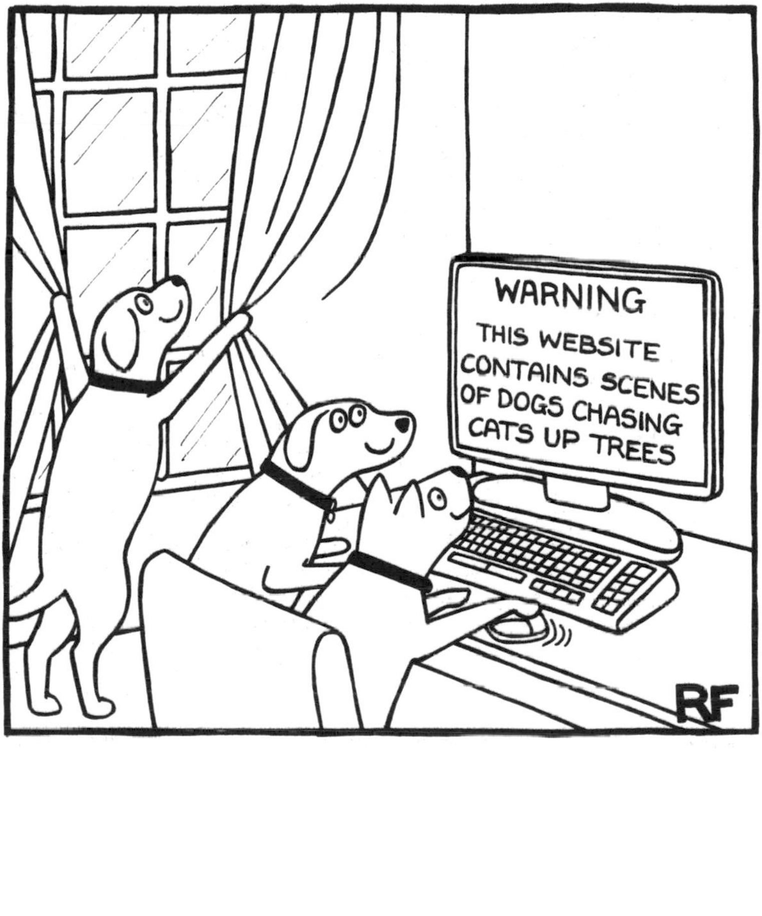
WARNING
THIS WEBSITE CONTAINS SCENES OF DOGS CHASING CATS UP TREES
RF

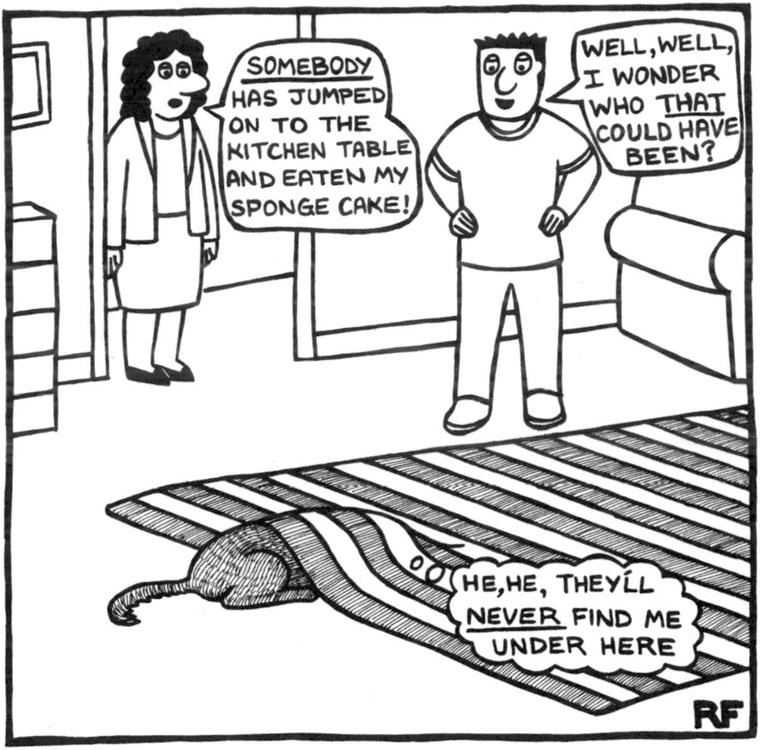
SOMEBODY HAS JUMPED ON TO THE KITCHEN TABLE AND EATEN MY SPONGE CAKE!
WELL, WELL, I WONDER WHO THAT COULD HAVE BEEN?
HE, HE, THEY'LL NEVER FIND ME UNDER HERE
RF

DADDY PUTS ON HIS WALKING BOOTS...

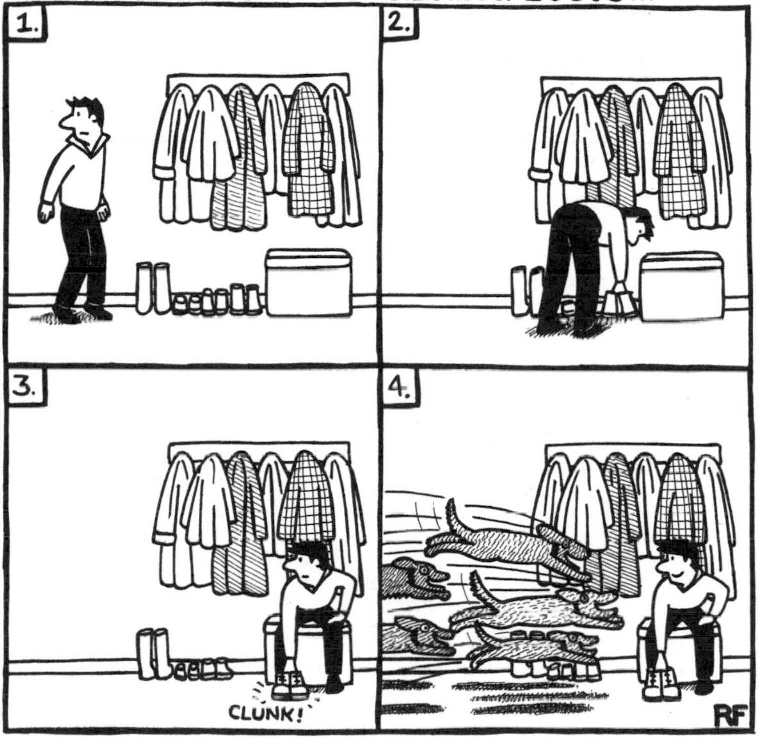
1.
2.
3.
CLUNK!
4.
RF

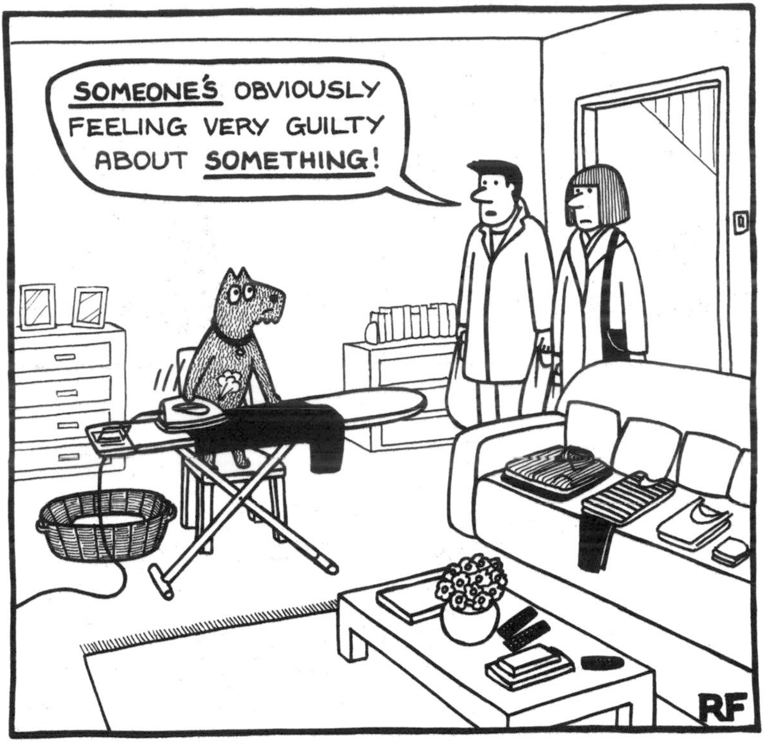
SOMEONE'S OBVIOUSLY FEELING VERY GUILTY ABOUT SOMETHING!
RF

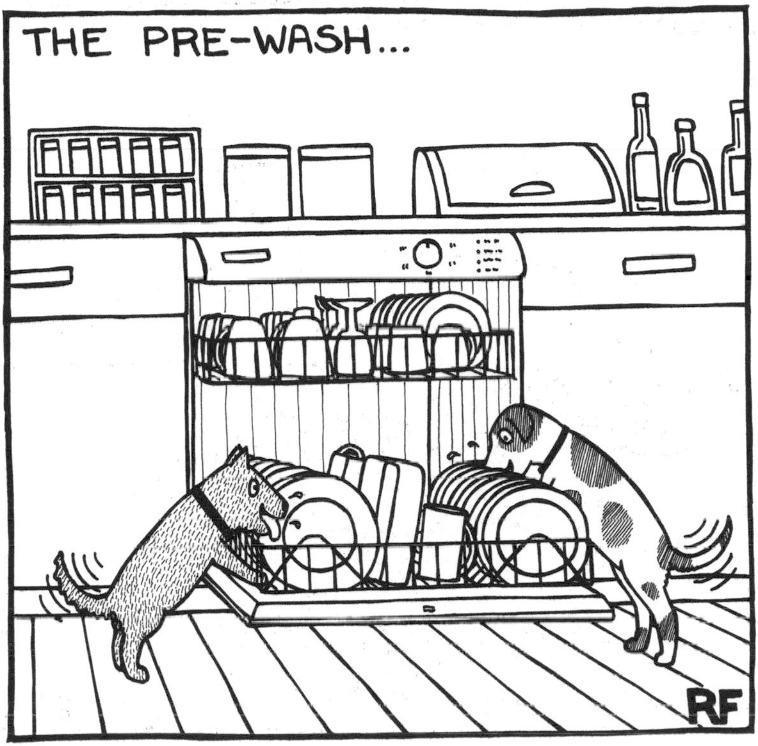
THE PRE-WASH...
RF

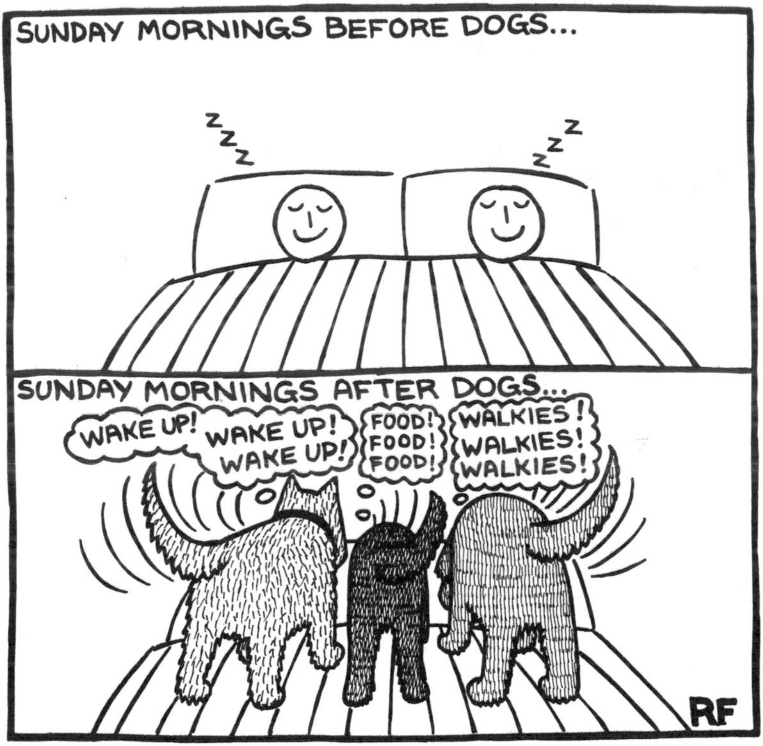
SUNDAY MORNINGS BEFORE DOGS...
ZZZ
ZZZ
SUNDAY MORNINGS AFTER DOGS...
WAKE UP!
WAKE UP! WAKE UP!
FOOD! FOOD! FOOD!
WALKIES! WALKIES! WALKIES!
RF

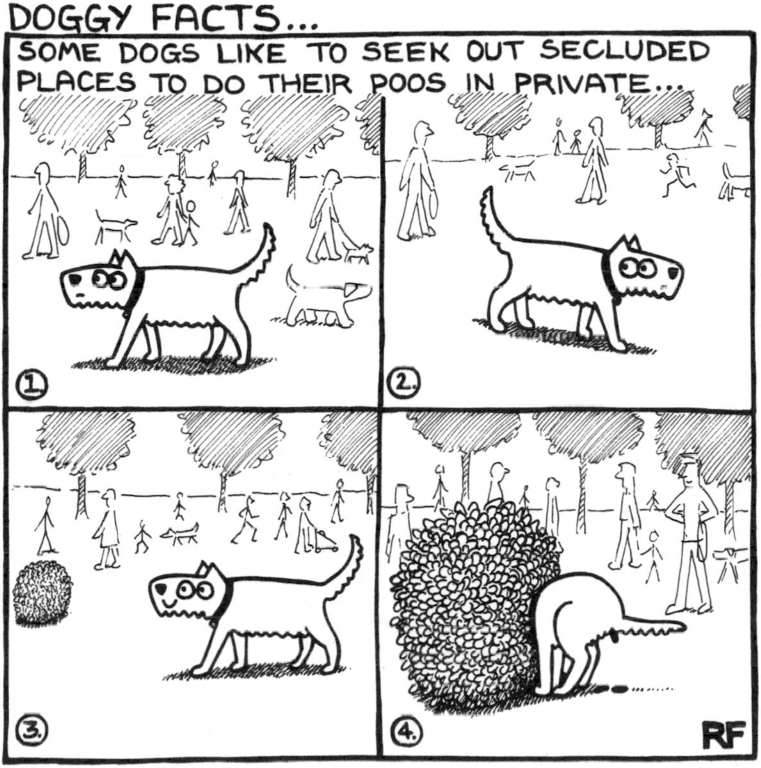
DOGGY FACTS...
SOME DOGS LIKE TO SEEK OUT SECLUDED PLACES TO DO THEIR POOS IN PRIVATE...
1.
2.
3.
4.
RF

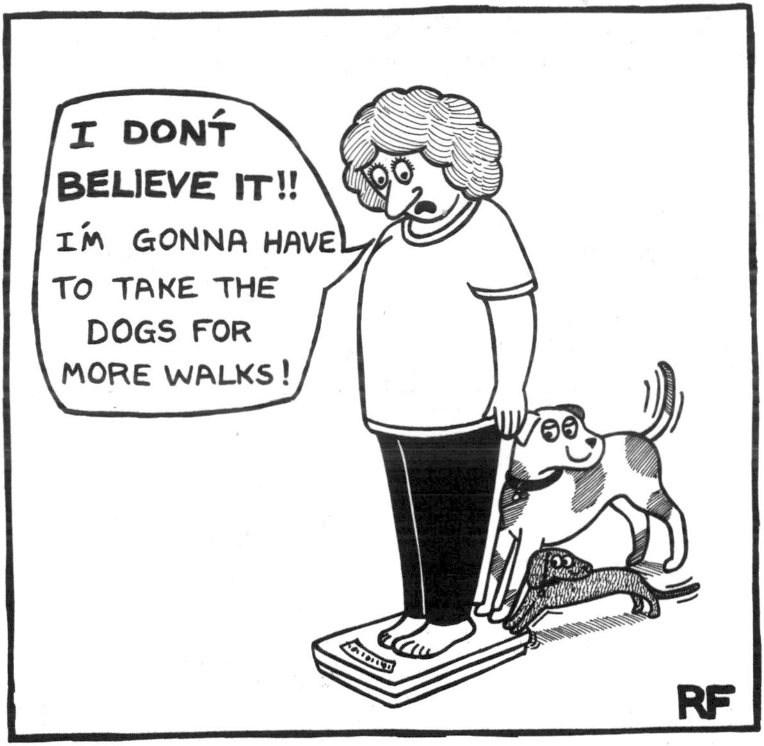
I DON'T BELIEVE IT!! I'M GONNA HAVE TO TAKE THE DOGS FOR MORE WALKS!
RF

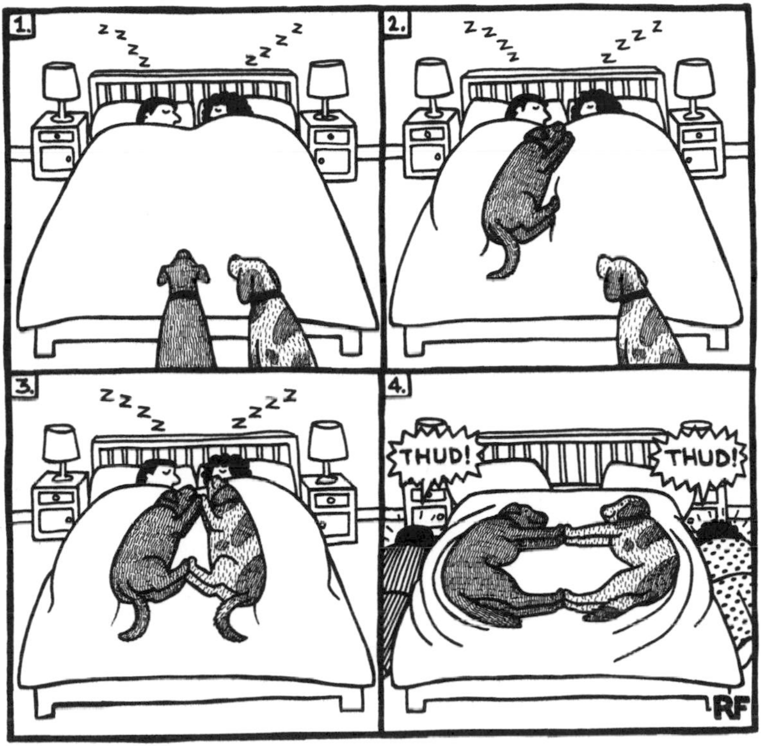
1.
ZZZZ
ZZZZ
2.
ZZZZ
ZZZZ
3.
ZZZZ
ZZZZ
4.
THUD!
THUD!
RF

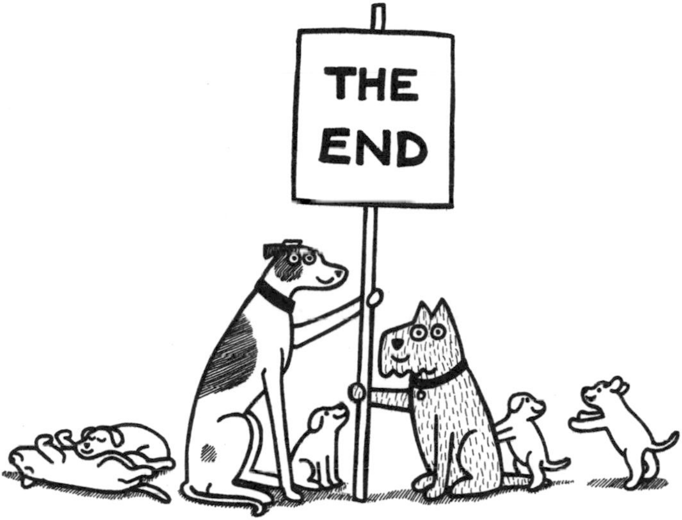
THE END

About the author

Rupert Fawcett became a professional cartoonist almost by accident when in 1989, whilst doodling, he drew a bald man in braces and carpet slippers and called him Fred. The Fred cartoons went on to be syndicated in the *Mail on Sunday* and published in several books. To date more than 9 million Fred greetings cards have been sold in the UK, Australia and New Zealand. Off The Leash is his latest creation.

www.rupertfawcettcartoons.com
www.offtheleashdogcartoons.com
www.facebook.com/OffTheLeashDailyDogCartoons